The Next Education Workforce

The Next Education Workforce

How Team-Based Staffing Models Can Support Equity and Improve Learning Outcomes

Carole G. Basile, Brent W. Maddin, and
R. Lennon Audrain

Co-Published in Partnership with
The American Superintendents Association

ROWMAN & LITTLEFIELD

Lanham • Boulder • New York • London

Published by Rowman & Littlefield
An imprint of The Rowman & Littlefield Publishing Group, Inc.
4501 Forbes Boulevard, Suite 200, Lanham, Maryland 20706
www.rowman.com

86-90 Paul Street, London EC2A 4NE, United Kingdom

British Library Cataloguing in Publication Information Available

Library of Congress Cataloging-in-Publication Data

Names: Basile, Carole G., 1958- author. | Maddin, Brent W., 1976- author. |
    Audrain, R. Lennon, 1999- author.
Title: The next education workforce : how team-based staffing models
    can support equity and improve learning outcomes / Carole G. Basile,
    Brent W. Maddin, R. Lennon Audrain.
Description: Lanham, Maryland : Rowman & Littlefield Publishing Group, 2023. |
    "Co-Published in Partnership with the National Association for Music
    Education." | Includes bibliographical references. | Summary: "The Next
    Education Workforce argues that the one-teacher, one-classroom model is
    outdated and suggests that schools should create teams of educators with
    distributed expertise who can deliver deeper and personalized learning
    experiences to all students. Steps to achieve this include offering actions to
    help facilitate sustainable systems change"—Provided by publisher.
Identifiers: LCCN 2022030141 (print) | LCCN 2022030142 (ebook) |
    ISBN 9781475867251 (cloth) | ISBN 9781475867268 (paperback) |
    ISBN 9781475867275 (epub)
Subjects: LCSH: Teaching teams. | Career education.
Classification: LCC LB1029.T4 B374 2023 (print) | LCC LB1029.T4 (ebook) |
    DDC 371.14/8—dc23/eng/20220810
LC record available at https://lccn.loc.gov/2022030141
LC ebook record available at https://lccn.loc.gov/2022030142

Contents

Foreword

It is not far-fetched to argue that democracy in the United States is dependent on the quality of its systems of public schooling. And if that is true, as I believe it is, then democracy in the United States is facing a crisis.

Criticism of public education, particularly its quality and costs, has existed ever since Horace Mann first began promoting schools that were free, enrolled boys and girls, and served children of every race and class. But in recent decades, critiques of America's public systems reached new levels of intensity. Prestigious figures from both political parties participated in wearing down the publics' support for its public schools. The myriad contemporary critiques of public education have given rise to a problem in education that was once local and often solvable: the problem of staffing our public schools.

Hiring qualified teachers for the classrooms of America's students is now quite difficult, in part because too many parents of college-educated children prefer that they *not* choose to be teachers. Parents say to their children, with some truth, that employment as a teacher lacks the prestige it once had. Further, the profession pays college-educated persons, particularly women, much too little. So, decades of criticism have now come home to roost! What used to be spot shortages of teachers—in rural and inner cities in particular—is now a national crisis of recruitment and retention of teachers. And this affects our democracy.

Around 50 million public school students a year need to be nurtured, socialized, educated, and prepared for both work and citizenship. Each cohort of students must learn subject matter as well as how to preserve America's political democracy and economic leadership. And to accomplish that, we believe we need a qualified teacher in every classroom. But with shrinking numbers of applicants for educational positions as we now know them, our goal may be impossible to meet.

In confronting that reality, we may want to ask, are the educational systems that we now have the only way to meet our national goals? And so, here is the reason to read this book. The authors present a thoughtful and exciting alternative to what we know to be the "tried and true" way to get an education, namely, a single teacher, with many students, working in one classroom. The proposals offered in this book may not only solve the staffing shortage, but they may also make for better education, provide for more culturally relevant education, and enhance the prestige of those in education who take on the role of lead teachers—those who provide the instructional wisdom for a team of professionals under the lead teachers' direction.

These authors invite you to create, with them, a new vision of public schooling. Their vision is clearly not written in stone. They invite other educators to develop their own game plans based on new models of how education for democracy and for the world of work can be accomplished. They seek a different model than the familiar one-teacher, one-classroom standard way of doing schooling, which is in use throughout all of American history.

In fact, this was the model in Plato's academy, in Victorian England, and in the overly romanticized one-room school-houses that were built throughout rural America. Although the one-teacher, one-classroom model of education has deep roots in all of the Western culture, it may be time for alternatives. A focus of this new model of doing school is the very sensible idea that teachers' expertise can be distributed: not every teacher needs to know everything about every subject matter, all the new technology, or each child and their families. But someone working with students should, indeed, know all these things!

I have been an educator for many years and am well aware that suggestions for rethinking schooling, in ways similar to the proposals in this book, are not new. But now, a shortage of trained career-seeking teachers, large number of students with special needs, increasing immigration bringing in culturally and linguistically varied students to our schools, and advanced and advancing technology make it more likely than ever before that a single teacher in a single classroom cannot do their job as well as could a team of educators working together. Thus, this is a most welcome book, asking all educators to rethink how we do schooling.

Can something like the ideas presented herein work? We sure won't know until some schools and school districts give it a try.

David C. Berliner
Regents Professor of Education, Emeritus
Arizona State University
Tempe, Arizona

Preface

For a long time, we have known that education would need to change if we were ever going to approach solving inequities and ensure that every learner is successful. Reform effort after reform effort, curriculum shifts, technology innovation, alternative teacher preparation and residencies, and a host of other programs have not moved the needle. Report after report bemoans the fact that disparities continue and that all learners are not being served in the ways that get them to the elusive goals our schools, districts, government agencies, think tanks, and others want them to achieve. We know that we need to address mental health, joyful learning, and quick and customized academic attention, and yet, we struggle—and we have struggled. Normal has needed to change for a long time.

And then in March of 2020, education did change—massively. Cracks in the normal festered and became bigger than we imagined. While we once thought this might be a blip on the screen—a lockdown and the pandemic would go away—we now recognize that learners and learning will be impacted for a long time. So, compounded by the pandemic, we hope this is the opportunity we have been waiting for—the kind of fundamental change we desperately need to provide the equitable practices learners need and deserve.[1] We believe this change begins with the educators: who they are, how they work together, and how their roles align to serve learners.

Most teachers are prepared and operate in one-teacher, one-classroom models as novices—sometimes with very little classroom teaching experience—and are expected to produce the same student outcomes as their veteran colleagues. Elementary teachers are often expected to teach all subjects to all students, and secondary teachers are often siloed into their content areas. Advancement in the profession, whether to pursue increased pay or a change in roles and responsibilities, typically requires teachers to leave the classroom into administrative and other supporting roles.

It is no surprise that we are facing what Wendy Robinson characterizes as an "impending crisis" in teacher recruitment, training, and retention.[2] For the first time in its history, the PDK Poll reported that over half of survey respondents would not want their own children to pursue teaching as a career.[3] These sentiments are mirrored in teacher preparation program enrollment as well. In 2018, enrollment in colleges of education had declined by more than one-third since 2010.[4]

This system is not only terrible for teachers as we have said; it's not working for learners. American student performance on national and international assessments is mediocre at best. Antiquated organizational features have left thousands of teachers and students behind, and thousands of teachers have left the field, leaving learners without high-quality educators. Efforts that focus only on recruiting, retention, or training are simply not enough. To ensure that we are getting the professional and learning outcomes that we want from education, we need to make a broad and deep commitment to systemic change.

That change begins with a recognition that the challenge is far more complex than a teacher shortage. As Peter Greene points out, a teacher shortage—alternatively labeled as a supply problem—rests on the premise that there are not enough qualified individuals to fill vacant teaching positions.[5] We have the quantity of qualified individuals that we need. This crisis in the education profession is not a teacher supply problem. The exodus from the profession, as well as the efficacy of the profession, is a function of how we have constructed the education workforce. It's a feature of the system, not a bug. In short, we face a workforce design problem.

This book is about designing and empowering the Next Education Workforce. While we certainly do not have all of this figured out and there are plenty of moving parts that need to change, we hope that this book sparks ideas about what those changes could look like. As we go to press, the COVID-19 pandemic, new arguments about long-standing social inequities, and a crisis of public trust in many inherited institutions and systems have created an exhausted education workforce.

Indeed, addressing these challenges will not be easy. Karl Popper and, later, Dave Snowden and Brenda Zimmerman talk about "clock and cloud" solutions.[6] Clock solutions are typically where we head first in education. We see a problem and we solve it with solutions that are predictable, controllable, and bounded—a new project, program, or activity (e.g., new curriculum, the latest technology, a recruitment or retention strategy). Rarely do such solutions address the root of the problem. Often, because they are frequently built on grants or other soft funding, they are not sustainable. Cloud solutions, however, are complex and focus on changing the structures, systems, and cultures of schools and schooling. Cloud solutions provide completely new and dynamic models and paradigm shifts.

Now is the time to make deep, more equitable changes in the ways that we prepare and deploy educators in learning environments. That's our focus here—on a cloud solution that is desirable not because it represents novelty and change for their own sake but because it allows us to build sustainable learning environments characterized by excellence and equity for both educators and learners.

NOTES

1. Audrain et al. (2022).
2. Robinson (2017, p. 2).
3. PDK International (2018).
4. Partelow (2019).
5. Greene (2019).
6. Ricigliano (2021).

Acknowledgments

We would like to thank our colleagues across Arizona State University's Mary Lou Fulton Teachers College and specifically Paul Gediman and the Next Education Workforce Team (Korbi Adams, Mary Brown, Natalie Nailor, Chelsea Nilsson, Kimberly Wright, and Lisa Wyatt) who contributed in ways big and small. Gratitude also goes to our school partners with whom we've been so fortunate to collaboratively build many of the concrete examples found throughout this book. To the countless colleagues, friends, and family who have pushed our thinking and offered feedback, we thank you.

Introduction

Human capital, the people who make up our education workforce, is at the heart of our learners' communities. These are the people who are responsible for building relationships and understanding the needs of every individual student; they are expected to know how to solve every learner's struggles and advance every learner's achievements. As a field, we have spent the last thirty years worrying about the quality of teachers and leaders and their relationship to the learning of students. We have sweat the details, compiling very detailed descriptions of all the things that teachers should know and be able to do.

As parents, we certainly want our kids to have teachers who have mastered all the competencies that we ask teachers to master. And, we'd probably want to add a bunch of other things to the list. However, as teacher educators, we have serious concerns about the ability of any single teacher to do all of those things well. The job of a teacher as currently designed, which asks each teacher to be all things to all learners, sets both educators and students up for failure. We believe that it is now time to redesign our education workforce.

In the past, the field of education has focused either on increasing teachers' instructional knowledge and skill (e.g., more and more professional learning) or increasing the level of complexity of the content students must learn (e.g., critical thinking and problem-solving), and sometimes both simultaneously. Rarely has the field sustained a fundamental rethinking of the roles that students and educators actually experience in learning environments or of the relationships among educators, students, and others that reside at the heart of learning. We must reexamine who we view as educators, how they work together, and how their collective and individual responsibilities should be defined.

What if we approach the long-standing problems of teacher shortage, educator diversity, lack of professional advancement, and other pressing challenges not as recruitment, retention, or even pipeline problems? What if, instead, we approach these issues as a workforce design problem—anchoring the challenge of what we think of as the Next Education Workforce in a commitment to

(1) provide all students with deeper and personalized learning by building teams of educators with distributed expertise and (2) empower educators by developing better ways to enter, specialize, and advance in the profession?

The phrase "Next Education Workforce" represents much more than simply the people who will staff schools. It represents a shift in how we design roles, deploy educators, and develop human capital in education. It's a commitment to building a better education workforce that allows for improved outcomes for educators and students.

To help us explore the Next Education Workforce, we've divided this book into two parts. We set the stage by examining ten currently "normal" ways of today's education. As it turns out, what passes for normal rests on a lot of assumptions that, when critically questioned, don't make much sense in the twenty-first century, especially given the inequities associated with today's educational systems.

In part I, we unpack the essential elements of the Next Education Workforce. We begin in chapter 2 by exploring the concept of teams with distributed expertise: Who makes up these teams? How are they organized? How do they share their expertise? In chapter 3, we turn our attention to deeper and personalized learning. While more student-centered learning has long been an aspiration in education, we believe that team-based models that leverage technology in new effective ways allow educators to deliver on a much broader set of student outcomes in ways that one-teacher, one-classroom staffing models cannot.

In chapter 4, we describe how Next Education Workforce models allow for new and better ways for educators to enter, specialize, and advance in the profession. These new pathways range from ways to integrate community members into teams to new formal credentialing routes for high school students and paraeducators. We see specialization as a means to distribute expertise and create new advancement pathways that keep educators in learning environments.

In chapter 5, we argue that the current one-teacher, one-classroom model actually fosters inequity for both students and educators. We believe that redesigning our education workforce allows us to begin to dismantle some of the systems and structures that passively and actively promote inequity. This section concludes with chapter 6, in which we spotlight what Next Education Workforce models look like in an elementary school, a high school, and a rural K–8 school.

Part II highlights three of the most important factors that allow Next Education Workforce models to launch and flourish. First among these is leadership at the system and school level, discussed in chapter 7. In chapter 8, we examine the role that teacher preparation and ongoing professional learning play in the success of Next Education Workforce models. In chapter 9, we look at how redesigning human capital management systems will be necessary to support sustainable solutions to many of the biggest challenges that school systems face.

In chapter 10, we note that building the Next Education Workforce is not an aspiration that can be left to the next generation to actualize. Rather, it's urgent work that hundreds of educators have already embraced. They have started building the Next Education Workforce. And so, we conclude with a call to action, inviting leaders, policymakers, educator preparers, and others to join that work immediately.

We recognize that these ideas are not exactly new. Many researchers, reformers, and others have written over the years about team-based models, differentiated staffing, teacher collaboration, distributed leadership, and deeper learning. But little of this work has generated enough traction to make it into actual schools at anything resembling scale. It's time to look at this work again, with a recognition that only by addressing deeply rooted systems and structures, rather than applying a series of programs and projects, can we effectively and sustainably improve educational outcomes and experience systems. We need to build the Next Education Workforce.

Chapter 1

Normal

School, in most places in the country and at most times, looks like school. Students sit in classrooms. Each classroom has one teacher. The teacher is expected to know everything that needs to be taught and to do everything for all students in the room. There are curriculum standards to follow, accountability measures to apply, and processes to assess the students, teachers, and the school itself. We are used to all of this. Regardless of your age, this probably sounds a lot like the school you attended. It is what we call normal. And maybe that consistency of schools makes us feel good and even provides some sense of stability in an uncertain world. However, it shouldn't.

As we began thinking about the Next Education Workforce, we started by looking at the systems and configurations of human capital in our schools that are typical and normal. Each of these aspects, at first glance, seem to make sense. After all, many are just how we've done things for decades. A second or third look, however, makes us shake our heads and wonder why schools do these things. Educators often learn and work in "normal" conditions that professionals in most other fields would not tolerate. Teachers and learners are both affected by these norms in significantly negative ways.

NORMAL 1: THE ONE-TEACHER, ONE-CLASSROOM MODEL

Today, the predominant model of staffing elementary schools is the one-teacher, one-classroom model. Every year, if you're a parent, you get an email announcing who your child's teacher is going to be. Typically, your perspective about the teacher is wholly derived from the information you have gathered from your neighbors and friends (or your own older child). You respond:

Yeah!, if it's the teacher everybody says is great;
Hmm, if it's the new teacher nobody knows; or
Argh!, if it's the teacher everybody says you really don't want.

There's no way to really know if that teacher is right for your child.

The more real, but subtle, problem is that, no matter how great the teacher might be, that teacher is still only one person and probably won't be the right teacher for everything an individual child needs, let alone all the things a group of twenty or more needs. While one-teacher, one-classroom models persist, one year of not having the right teacher can make an incredible difference in influencing and determining a child's future—a fact that is even more true for families without financial means to remediate or complement less than ideal schooling.

This one-teacher, one-classroom model—the fundamental structure of schools—locks us into a normal, that, if really considered, forces education to forfeit so many opportunities to provide equitable learning environments for students, more satisfying working conditions for teachers, and better outcomes for both.

NORMAL 2: SUBSTITUTE TEACHERS

Not only does the one-teacher, one-classroom model fail to meet the needs of all learners, it also creates optimal conditions for a daily crisis across 3.1 million U.S. classrooms. If a teacher is absent—whether for a few hours, a day, a week; or on sick leave, family leave, or some other leave—the school must find someone to staff that classroom. This is also true when the school can't staff a position and requires a long-term stand-in. Normally, the solution is a substitute teacher.

Illness, family emergencies, in-service training requirements, and pandemics—these things happen. An average teacher in the United States is absent for these and other reasons nearly eleven days out of any given school year. That's between 5 and 6 percent of the school year. Usually that 5 or 6 percent is covered by a substitute teacher.[1]

Under the best conditions, classroom teachers know when they'll be out, craft detailed plans for known substitutes (who may even be educators who retired from that school), and empower the students to drive their own learning. But best conditions are not the norm.

Typically, if a school can even find a substitute (which only happens about 80 percent of the time),[2] that substitute has no professional teaching experience and will have received fewer than four hours of training. Even when substitutes have been trained and have experience, students often learn a fraction of what they normally would, and, too often, classroom safety suffers. Just type "substitute teacher cartoon" into a search engine and you'll get a pretty good depiction of what is normal with substitutes. Yet, still, this is our normal go-to option when schools are missing a teacher.

NORMAL 3: LOCKSTEP LEARNERS

No one learns at the same pace and in the same way. Education knows this, and so our education system asks teachers to provide individualized instruction, differentiated learning experiences, and multitiered levels of support to their students. Yet, most of our educational systems are built on the assumption that learners are identical and that their progress is measured on a narrow set of outcomes based on this assumption. In our age-graded and standardized systems, all students are expected to achieve the same knowledge and skills by the end of each school year. Another "normal" question is, "Can education reasonably ask any one teacher to manage the complexity of individualized and differentiated learning experiences for an entire classroom full of students?"

Simply put, this is unreasonable to ask of a single teacher. A few teachers may go to herculean lengths to meet the needs of all learners and are held up as what is possible. But at what cost? Many others often "teach to the middle" and worry about where they are relative to a pacing guide—which often yields frustrated learners and teachers alike. To make the work of teaching easier for teachers in a one-teacher, one-classroom model, schools expect each student to work on the same activity, topic, or content as every other student in the room: schools expect widget learners, moving through a curriculum in lockstep.

Expecting widget learners stifles both teacher and learner agency. Teachers are unable to utilize their expertise to provide the right

learning experiences at the right time for students because they are
working with too many students with different needs. Students are
unable to achieve their personalized potentials because they all have
different learning trajectories and needs, their interests are not piqued,
and their strengths are not utilized.

NORMAL 4: WHAT EDUCATION MEASURES

There is a misalignment between what people think the purpose of
schooling is and what is measured in educational settings. Ask parents,
educators, and other members from the community what they believe
the purpose of schooling is and you're likely to get a range of answers:
"To prepare students for college and the world of work," "to become
positive, contributing citizens in our democracy," "to learn how to
learn," or "to lead choice-filled lives." There are a host of broader student outcomes that are worthy of consideration and measurement.

Our point here isn't to say that learning content isn't important. We
think it is, and we think it should be measured. But the point is to argue
that, in addition to measuring the things education has for the last few
decades, education should broaden the scope of its metrics to better
align with the sorts of answers people give to the question, what is the
purpose of schooling?

NORMAL 5: WIDGET TEACHERS

As a society, we want a quality teacher in every classroom, but the
work of teaching is complex. In the current one-teacher, one-classroom
model, teachers in every classroom need to be able to do everything:
plan lessons and align them with curricula and standards; deliver
instruction; assess the learning of batches of students and be responsible
for their learning progress; and continue professional development.

The list of what is asked of teachers to do keeps growing—from
preventing cyberbullying to teaching with trauma-informed practices
to running engaging, fully online classes. Many have written about the
plight of the "widget" effect, which is what happens when school systems assume teacher talent and effectiveness are the same from teacher
to teacher,[3] but the education system views them as normal. But how is

it possible to be effective at an ever-expanding set of responsibilities? It's not.

NORMAL 6: THE SCHOOL LEADER AS INSTRUCTIONAL EXPERT

Since the 1970s, the focus of educational leadership programs has been on improving school and classroom instruction. Instructional leadership heavily centers on the principal. Traditionally, engaged instructional leaders are hands-on about curriculum and instruction and work directly with teachers. Since many educational leaders have been classroom teachers themselves, their beliefs about students and learning are influenced by their own experiences, most likely in one-teacher, one-classroom models.

Moving past beliefs, in most schools, the principal is the direct supervisor of all of the teachers and also serves as the instructional leader. In this sense, they are expected to support each educator's individual professional growth as well as stay up-to-date on all aspects of teaching and learning. They are asked to do all this while also being responsible for setting the overall vision for the school, maintaining an overall positive culture and climate, and working with families and the community. School leadership is invariably difficult because the organizational structure of schools today doesn't lend itself to the practices we know support leaders and strengthen the overall organization.

NORMAL 7: ONE-SIZE-FITS-ALL TEACHER PREPARATION AND PROFESSIONAL LEARNING

Teacher preparation is between a rock and a hard place. While teacher preparation might want to prepare our teacher candidates for new models and new structures, it continues to be bound by the actual working environments our graduates are entering: the one-teacher, one-classroom model.

Everything teacher preparation does—its content, its instructional methodologies, its clinical experiences—is based on assumptions that incentivize it to produce "widget teachers" who all know and are able to do the same things. We think of this as "preparing teachers for infinity."

Because teacher preparation doesn't know the exact context in which novice teachers will begin working, it prepares them for as many possibilities as it can. At its worst, this can lead to box-checking around professional standards—trying to simply "cover" as much as possible.

Similarly, school systems, rooted in the one-teacher, one-classroom model, often ask that all educators complete the same professional training. In an era when more schools are thinking about personalized learning for students, shouldn't we think about personalizing the training of educators? One-teacher, one-classroom models do not provide the infrastructure to support collaboration and continuous improvement within schools for any of these adults and, as a result, educators face isolation and inflexibility. The one-size-fits-all approach to teacher preparation and professional learning reflects a system that values compliance over successful creativity. It's a terrible way to educate learners and a terrible way to develop and retain educators.

NORMAL 8: FIRST-YEAR TEACHERS ALONE IN CLASSROOMS BY THEMSELVES

As complex and difficult as the work of teaching is, it is a wonder that schools place rookie, day-one teachers in classrooms by themselves. But schools do. Not only do schools place them by themselves, but schools typically expect these recently inducted teachers to achieve the same student outcomes as their more experienced teacher colleagues. Yes, schools often provide mentors to novices, but the quality of mentorship varies greatly. Evidence points to the fact that most teachers don't begin to plateau in terms of efficacy until their fifth year on the job,[4] which, coincidentally, is also when almost half (44 percent) of new teachers will have left the profession.[5]

At the beginning of books, induction programs, or professional development designed for new teachers, there's often a graphic. It shows the "first year teaching roller coaster." The teacher is on a rollercoaster from the beginning of the school year until the end. The teacher moves from anticipation to survival to disillusionment to rejuvenation to reflection and back to anticipation.

While we would like to believe that novice teachers rejuvenate and survive year after year, many do not. In any event, under what circumstances is it okay that, in October, so many teachers are sitting in their cars crying in disillusionment? Why should the first year of teaching be about survival? Why has novice teachers' navigation of first-year teaching experiences been described as sink-or-swim? Why has it been the norm to put teachers, alone, into classrooms and expect them to achieve the same student outcomes as their veteran teacher counterparts?

NORMAL 9: HUMAN RESOURCE SYSTEMS MAINTAIN SCHOOL SYSTEMS, NOT LEARNING SYSTEMS

Many human resource systems (i.e., hiring processes, pay structures, evaluation systems, and labor contracts) are often disconnected from learning systems, making it hard to know whether schools have recruited and retained the right individuals, based on what students need. When hiring, principals must sift through piles of applicants that meet generic criteria (degree in elementary education), rather than receiving a list of potential candidates that have the expertise to meet the needs of the particular learners in their particular schools.

Current teacher evaluation systems perpetuate the one-teacher, one-classroom model by incentivizing individuals for their students' achievement without acknowledging that other educators also likely had an impact on those learners—whether that be paraeducators in elementary contexts or other subject teachers at the secondary level. Additionally, human resource systems often do not incentivize specialization and advancement opportunities that help guide educators in their own professional learning or insure that the best educators have the greatest impact on learning.

NORMAL 10: LEARNERS HAVE LIMITED ACCESS TO THE ADULTS THEY NEED

As a society, we've long held on to the myth that students only need one good teacher or one good mentor. The truth is, those learners who have experienced the most success have had multiple adults in their lives providing what they need when they need it. Schools have some specialists—counselors, special educators, reading specialists, multi-language learner supports, and maybe even an occupational therapist.

Yet, all of those specialists have large caseloads, and their services are typically pull-out rather than push-in. This approach removes students from the central learning environment rather than including the support they need in the default environment. It stigmatizes certain learning needs and excludes some learners from what is considered "normal."

Schools also haven't done a good job of recognizing the vast assets of our communities and intentionally making them part of students' formal education. School systems create a myriad of requirements and fees that dissuade people from volunteering in schools, and too many policies make it difficult for schools to bring in members of the community as part-time or even paid educators. Schools say that these people cannot be alone with students without a professional educator in the room.

However, after the last bell has rung, the community embraces the same individuals as they run private music lessons, host youth organization meetings in their homes, or coach youth soccer teams. Students are learning, getting mentored, and receiving all sorts of support outside of the formal school day. What would happen if schools reduced the barriers that prevent talented, caring adults in our communities from contributing formally to the learning that happens in our schools?

CONTEXT MATTERS

We talk about Next Education Workforce models in the plural, as opposed to a one-size-fits-all model, because context matters. This work looks different from school to school and from community to community. The composition of the teams of educators and the specific skills and areas of expertise has to be determined to meet the needs of each specific group of learners and the curriculum in which they engage. There is no rigid timeline for this work. It must move at the speed of trust among all those involved—parents, educators, administrators, and others.

But we also know that we simply can't wait any longer. We are continuing to place difficult demands on our education systems and on our educators. We need solutions that are equally good for teachers and learners. In 2020, the Education Commission stated the following:

> We have no time to waste. Now is the time for all actors—and most importantly policymakers and members of the education workforce

themselves—to be open to new ways of working and learning together. It takes a team to educate a child. By building learning teams and learning systems, we can harness the human and social capital of the wider workforce and create a learning generation.[6]

After decades of school reform, the structure or systems of education have changed very little. This is acutely true of the ways in which teachers function and the roles they play. Technology is upon us like never before, and the world is changing too quickly for the one-teacher, one-classroom model where a teacher needs to know and be able to do everything learners need them to do. It's just not sustainable.

CONCLUSION

In this chapter, we've summarized what the normative model of schooling looks like for students, teachers, and systems leaders. The rest of the book is dedicated to an exploration of how the Next Education Workforce can help build a next normal. We believe the Next Education Workforce can help build a next normal in which learners and teachers escape the one-teacher, one-classroom model, in which learning is personal and developmental, and in which no teacher, substitute, novice, or community educator works in a classroom by themselves.

We envision a next normal in which teachers are not treated like widgets; school leaders are asked and empowered to be systems-level leaders; teacher preparation embraces specialization; professional learning means acquiring new competencies; human resources are deployed to improve learning; and learners are surrounded by adults who can provide the expertise they need when they need it. Ultimately, our objective is to create better working conditions for teachers and learning conditions, experiences, and outcomes for students—because the normative model of schooling that we've had for decades is simply not working.

NOTES

1. Northern (2020).
2. Vialet & von Moos (2020).

3. Weisberg et al. (2009).
4. Kane et al. (2008).
5. Ingersoll et al. (2018).
6. Education Commission (2020, p. 4).

Part I

ELEMENTS OF THE NEXT EDUCATION WORKFORCE

Chapter 2

Teams of Educators and Distributed Expertise

In healthcare, each nurse or doctor isn't expected to know everything. In law firms, there are teams of lawyers and paralegals who work together to research and provide legal services. Accounting and auditing firms utilize teams with differing expertise. Engineers, social service providers, university administrators, business analysts, technology specialists, and chefs—just about everyone—work in teams. But teachers rarely do.

You might say that teachers are already working in teams, whether that be in professional learning communities, data teams, co-teaching teams, or departmental or grade-level teams. However, these aren't the kind of teams we are talking about. Teachers may work together, plan together, and look at data together, but they inevitably go back to their classroom, shut the door, and work by themselves during that critical time when they are working directly with students. Sometimes there's a paraeducator in the classroom. Sometimes a volunteer, co-teacher, or specialist drops in to help with particular students. But rarely are these relationships truly team based in a way that is both collaborative and coordinated.

Every learner needs a collaborative team. We can no longer take a group of students, allot twenty-five to thirty students to a classroom, and then expect that that one teacher can meet all of their students' needs. It's time to take groups of students, analyze their needs, and build a team of educators around them.

The idea of bringing teams of educators around groups of students is not a new one. Educational historian Larry Cuban describes team teaching as an educational best practice that "flew across the educational sky in the 1960s and disappeared by the mid-1970."[1] In 1968, Lloyd Trump and Delmas Miller defined educator teams as

> an arrangement in which two or more teachers and their assistants, taking advantage of their respective competencies, plan, instruct, and evaluate in one or more subject areas a group of elementary or secondary students equivalent in size to two or more conventional classes, using a variety of technical aids to teaching and learning through large group instruction, small group discussions, and independent study.[2]

This is the definition we subscribe to throughout the book and in our discussion of the elements and benefits of developing the Next Education Workforce. While anchored in the past, we believe that it is time to revisit the concept of educator teams given advances in technology, the return to more student-centered learning models, and the current and impending challenges of staffing schools.

BUILDING BLOCKS OF EDUCATOR TEAMS

It turns out that most of what schools need to build high-quality educator teams is already available to them. There are four major types of educators that currently exist in most of our systems:

- *Educational leaders* include teacher leaders, school leaders, and systems leaders who are accountable for the academic and socio-emotional growth of students and responsible for the deployment, performance, and professional growth of other educators.
- *Professional educators* include preservice, novice, experienced, and specialist teachers who are accountable for students' academic and socio-emotional growth.
- *Paraeducators* include instructional assistants, teaching assistants, and other school employees whose knowledge and skills complement those of professional educators.
- *Community educators* include classified staff, substitutes, volunteers, and other community members whose knowledge and skills complement those of professional educators.

Think of these as the building blocks of human capital. If you look deeper into any of these educator types, you'll discover important differences in expertise, strengths, and requisite training. The hallmark of Next Education Workforce teams is that they are made up of individuals drawn from these educator types and deployed in new roles with specific responsibilities that play to educators' strengths and level of preparation. In doing so, it is possible to better meet the needs of students in specific learning environments while simultaneously creating jobs that are rewarding and accessible to a greater number of educators.

CORE AND EXTENDED TEAMS

Before digging more deeply into the importance of distributed expertise in team-based models and how roles might vary and complement one another, it is helpful to first describe how school systems are organizing educators into teams. We think about the team in two different ways: the core team and the extended team.

Members of the core team typically work with the same, shared roster of students for a sustained period of time. Often this is a full year; however, in some cases, it may only be a semester, depending on the school's schedule. A core team shares responsibility for students' academic and socio-emotional growth. This group meets regularly—often daily—to co-plan, look at student work, and discuss what changes are needed to the upcoming schedule to best meet learner needs. The actual composition of educators on a core term varies as a function of context but typically includes an educational leader (e.g., team lead), several professional educators, and sometimes paraeducators and preservice teachers (e.g., teacher residents).

The extended team includes educators who provide additional support to students and the core team. Members of the extended team may work across multiple teams at a school, or even across schools—especially if they are specialists or elective teachers. Community educators are almost always members of the extended team. Whether paraeducators are members of the core or extended team is a matter of context and is likely to be a function of how many total core teams a paraeducator supports and how many hours a week they work.

Consider how an elementary school and a high school organized their educators onto core and extended teams:

Elementary School (third-grade team, 100 students):

- *Core Team*: Three certified teachers (one of whom leads the team), three preservice teachers (residents, working five days a week), and a paraeducator.
- *Extended Team*: Several elective teachers, a media specialist, a Title I specialist, and a special educator, all of whom are working across multiple teams.

High School (ninth-grade team, 150 students):

- *Core Team*: Biology teacher (who also serves as the lead teacher), a math teacher, an English teacher, a career and technical education teacher, and a special educator.
- *Extended Team*: Remote math teachers (who supplement math instruction), an English Language Learner educator (shared across multiple teams), several elective teachers, and community educators from local industry who serve as project-based mentors.

Again, it is important to note that schools design educator teams in all sorts of ways.

Both of the aforementioned examples describe teams organized around a grade level, but we have partner schools, even within the same district, that have designed teams that serve multi-age learners (e.g., grades 3, 4, and 5). There are some teams that only have two professional educators on the core team and others that have five. Some teams have lead teachers, others have opted to not. Sometimes there are very large extended teams, and sometimes it's just the core team. What they all have in common is that there are at least two professional teachers who share a common (almost always, larger) roster of students, and the educators are taking advantage of their distributed expertise to better meet the needs of their students and make the job of teaching more accessible and sustainable.

DISTRIBUTING EXPERTISE

The success of team-based staffing models relies on the fact that educators—leaders, teachers, paraeducators, and community educators—all have valuable forms of expertise. Simply putting educators on teams isn't enough. Schools need to strategically build educator teams that distribute expertise so that the right educators are engaged in the right tasks at the right time to produce wildly better results for both students and the educator team.

The World Health Organization has been talking about "task-shifting" for decades in healthcare settings to strengthen and deliver healthcare services more effectively.[3] The approach involves moving specific tasks from highly qualified healthcare workers (i.e., doctors and nurses) and redistributing them to "workers with shorter training and fewer qualifications in order to make more efficient use of the available human resources for health" (i.e., technicians).[4] Moving specific tasks from highly trained healthcare workers with broad expertise to a range of workers with different specific areas of preparation exhibited the potential to reduce costs without compromising the outcomes for patients.[5]

Task shifting provides a way to reconsider traditional educator roles and create new ones. Like the examples in medicine, it is possible to take the ever-expanding list of responsibilities of teachers and leaders in monolithic roles and think about how those tasks could be redistributed among an educator team. Importantly, this doesn't just mean taking the tasks that professional educators don't want to do and giving them to another member of the team who may have less training or status. Instead, it requires asking who is the best person on the team to do a particular aspect of this very complicated job and if they don't have the capacity, what could be shifted to someone else to allow for that?

When thinking about who on a team should know what, we expect educational leaders and professional educators to have baseline areas of knowledge. For example, every elementary teacher needs to have a basic understanding of mathematics and how to teach mathematics. A team, however, may have a lead math planner who is responsible for examining data, general planning and grouping, and making recommendations for personalizing the instruction for students.

At the secondary level, secondary science teachers need a deep understanding of their content, but it may be that someone on the team has applied knowledge from industry, deeper understanding of problem- or project-based learning, or a deeper knowledge of technology integration. When placed on teams, teachers are no longer isolated and expected to be experts in all things, at all times, for all students. Rather, there is distributed expertise, and educators can collaborate and coordinate with one another to develop and deliver deeper and more personalized learning experiences to students.

Task shifting is also powerful when considering novice teachers, paraeducators, and community educators. In current one-teacher, one-classroom staffing models, these educators are often either underutilized or asked to do far more than for which they are adequately prepared. In team-based models, they can take on specific parts of the job for which they are prepared and upskill in specific areas (e.g., reading instruction, assessment, and supporting struggling learners) that will allow them to take on new aspects of the work.

An example will help show the power of distributing expertise in a team-based staffing model. Table 2.1 shows two staffing models for a third grade with 100 students. Although contrived, this example is representative of many of the elementary schools with whom we partner. We could have just as easily created an example based on our secondary school partners and encourage you to see chapter 6 where we describe three different school models, including a K-8 school and a high school, in much greater detail.

In the one-teacher, one-classroom model depicted in table 2.1, the students are spread across four classrooms and are taught by four educators that vary in their years of experience and pathway into the profession.

- *Teacher A*: National Board Certified Teacher with fifteen years of experience and a master's degree in special education.
- *Teacher B*: Former engineer who entered through an alternative pathway and has five years of experience.
- *Teacher C*: First-year teacher who graduated from local teacher prep program.
- *Long-Term Substitute*: Recent college grad with a BA in English.
- *Paraeducator*: Parent with a high school diploma who has children at the school.

In this example, and increasingly common in many schools, a long-term substitute (or an emergency credentialed teacher) is the teacher of record for one of the classes. The two columns in table 2.1 show how educators' responsibilities might shift as a school moves from a one-teacher, one-classroom staffing model to a team-based model.

Table 2.1   Shifting Educator Responsibilities in a Third-Grade Context

	One-Teacher, One-Classroom Model	Team-Based Model
Students	• *Class A*: twenty-five students, seven students with IEPs • *Class B*: twenty-five students, eight students with IEPs • *Class C*: twenty-five students • *Class D*: twenty-five students ~twenty students are multilingual learners	• All 100 of the same students are on a single, shared roster • Team of educators shares responsibility for their academic and socio-emotional growth
Teacher A	All four educators are responsible for • Planning math, ELA, science, social studies • Communicating with parents • Meeting students' SEL needs • Managing class website and tech • Supervising recess and dismissal • And LOTS of other things	• Lead teacher duties (makes schedule, deploys team based on data, member of school leadership team, observation+feedback for team) • Head ELA planner • Teaches larger-group ELA and math lessons • Targeted support for fifteen students with IEPs
Teacher B		• Head math planner • Chief communicator with families • Teaches ELA, math, science, and social studies
Teacher C		• Head science & social studies planner • Manages class website and tech • Coordinates community educators • Teaches ELA, math, science, and social studies
Long-Term Substitute		• Administers all reading diagnostics • Supports small groups during ELA, math, science, and social studies • Leads fifteen-minute mindfulness sessions • Assists with recess and pickup

(continued)

Table 2.1 (Continued)

	One-Teacher, One-Classroom Model	Team-Based Model
Paraeducator	Largely works with fifteen students with IEPs who are in Classes A and B	• Serves as a student success coach for twenty historically underserved learners • Facilitates all online learning experiences for students (e.g., adaptive math software). • Supervises recess and pickup
Community Educators	Do not systematically exist in this model	• Retired teachers work with small reading groups five hours/week (paid) • College students tutor math three hours/week (paid) • Engineers from local businesses one time a week as project-based mentors (volunteer) • Team of ten family members help with dismissal each day (volunteer)

Importantly, the shifts described in the table represent relatively straightforward changes to this school's third-grade staffing model. For the most part, no new roles were created; the existing human capital from the one-teacher, one-classroom model was just organized differently and responsibilities were shifted to better meet the students' needs and make the job more rewarding for educators. While there are lots that could be unpacked in table 2.1, we want to call attention to shifts experienced by four particular educators in this model: the experienced teacher, the first-year teacher, the paraeducator, and the substitute teacher.

Expanding the Impact of Experienced and Effective Teachers

As schools build team-based staffing models, new opportunities emerge for experienced and effective teachers to expand their impact on both students and other educators. In the one-teacher, one-classroom model described in table 2.1, the National Board Certified teacher (Teacher A) works with the same number of students as the other third-grade teachers and likely has a limited impact on their professional growth and development. However, in the team-based model, Teacher A can take on responsibilities for leading the team and all 100 third-grade students benefit from the direct support, planning, and leadership of this individual.

Schools with whom we've partnered have created various titles for experienced and effective educators assuming these responsibilities. In this book, we will call them "lead teachers." They facilitate team meetings and determine how educators—professional, para, and community—can best be deployed given the needs of the students and the strengths of the team. Lead teachers often also become the instructional leaders on the team, and principals can shift responsibilities for observation, feedback, and other educator support to these individuals.

School systems either create new formal roles for lead teachers or create stipends or other incentives (e.g., additional planning time) to recognize their expertise and increased responsibility. In doing so, systems are also creating advancement opportunities for their best teachers that don't stop them from working directly with students or require them to leave the classroom. For those educators interested in school or system leadership opportunities, the job of leading an educator team allows them to develop the knowledge, skills, and dispositions associated with success in future leadership positions. This helps develop a bench of future leaders in the long term and actively retains our most effective and experienced educators in the short term.

Humanely Inducting Novice Teachers into the Profession

In the one-teacher, one-classroom model, first-year teachers like Teacher C from table 2.1 have essentially the same set of responsibilities as veteran educators. Anyone who has worked with novice teachers knows that they range widely in effectiveness, even if they have graduated from the same teacher preparation program. More importantly, we also know that they each have unique areas of strength and expertise. Some may be excellent at planning hands-on mathematics lessons using the latest technology; others may be experts in building trusting relationships with students and family. Some may be able to do both well. Yet, we treat every novice the same—giving them the keys to their own classrooms and copies of first-year teacher "survival guides," and we hope that they will be great at everything.

However, when placed on a team of educators, novice teachers no longer need to be good at everything (nor does any other educator on the team). They can still positively contribute in deep and meaningful ways but only in the areas where they will be most successful or with a reduced set of responsibilities allowing them to do fewer things better. In the team-based model described earlier, Teacher C still helps teach all four subjects but has only planning responsibilities for science and social studies.

Additionally, they lead the communication with families and the integration of technology into all lessons—presumably skills that this teacher possesses and, also importantly, allows other educators to not focus on these areas. With time, continued professional learning, and lots of modeling from other educators on the team, Teacher C will continue to broaden their skills, refine their craft, and take on more complicated aspects of the job.

Creating Meaningful Jobs and Pathways for Paraeducators

Paraeducators, sometimes known as teachers' aides or instructional assistants, are often underutilized or asked to support students in ways that far exceed their professional training. Like the paraeducator from table 2.1, they often support students with special needs in inclusive classroom settings. While the requirements for being a paraeducator differ from state to state, under the Every Student Succeeds Act (ESSA) paraeducators must hold at least a high school diploma and (1) have finished two years of college or technical school, (2) hold at least an associate's degree, or (3) take a state or local assessment of their ability to assist in reading, wring, and math instruction.[6]

The lack of adequate (or any) preparation for paraeducators, coupled with the fact that they are often working students, who have some of the most complex learning and socio-emotional needs means that their impact may be limited and their job may be more challenging than it needs to be.

In the United States, there are over 1.3 million paraeducators[7] who could be deployed differently. Team-based staffing models allow para-educators to assume different roles and prepare for those specific roles. As shown in table 2.1, the paraeducator becomes a member of the core team and takes on three key responsibilities—serving as a student success coach for twenty at-risk students, serving as a learning lab facilitator when students are learning online, and supervising recess and pickup. Central to each of these responsibilities is building deep and trusting relationships with students as well as mastering a few technical skills for which professional learning should be available.

Reframing Substitutes as Members of a Community Educator Workforce

Substitutes represent a massively underutilized part of the education workforce—more than 600,000 strong. Almost none receive any formal training[8]—unless, of course, they were trained as professional teach-ers, but that's not often the case. Today, most substitutes walk cold into a classroom of twenty-plus students and are expected to maintain order and, hopefully, advance learning. The lack of preparation is more problematic when an underqualified substitute is responsible for much longer periods of instruction (e.g., covering family leave or when a school can't staff a position), as is the case for the long-term substitute from table 2.1 in the one-teacher, one-classroom model.

In team-based models, where the roster of students is shared among professional educators, a team can rearrange the schedule and students when a colleague is out for a day, even on short notice. While not ideal, the disruption to classroom culture and student learning is far less severe in a team-based model. Because of this, some schools that we work with have eliminated budget lines for substitutes entirely and redeployed those monies in other ways (e.g., stipends for lead teachers, part-time community educator contracts).

When an educator is out for a prolonged period of time or cannot be hired, it is still possible to hire a person into the team-based model. However, this person is not "substituting" for the professional educator, but rather, they are taking on specific and appropriate responsibilities on the team. As described in table 2.1, the long-term substitute in the team-based model (who happens to have a bachelor's degree in English) takes on the administration of all reading diagnostics (presumably with training), supports small groups during content blocks, leads daily mindfulness sessions, and assists the paraeducator with recess and pickup duties.

This person, and all substitutes working in team-based models, should be reconsidered as community educators. They are caring adults who have already signaled an interest in working in schools and have come to the team with specific skills and interests that should be leveraged. For those who are retired educators or those who have temporarily left the profession, team-based models provide new and interesting opportunities to engage in part-time roles. For others, like the school's classified staff or individuals from local business and industry, they bring specific content knowledge and expertise that most professional educators lack.

Rather than upskilling our professional educators, schools should better leverage the distributed expertise of community educators. Table 2.1 highlights a few ways in which community educators—including retired educators, college tutors, local engineers, and families—could complement the work of the educational team.

Unlocking the Power of Educator Teams

The example described in table 2.1 is, by design, straightforward. Our hope is that school and systems leaders can look at the team-based model and think, "We could put that into action next year." Schools with which we partner have simply taken the existing human capital working in a one-teacher, one-classroom model and deployed them as an educator team, shifting responsibilities in ways that made sense given the educators' expertise. With the exception of the lead teacher position and maybe the community educators, schools didn't create any new roles. Many of the schools start in the same way—with a single educator team, using the existing human capital and no new roles, at a single grade level.

As schools move beyond the first year of implementation and especially as they add more teams at the school (or across schools), much more interesting possibilities for grouping students, educator roles, and distributing expertise begin to emerge. Some schools have gravitated toward multi-age teams (e.g., teams serving third, fourth, and fifth graders or seventh and eighth graders). Some have experimented with vertical teams within a subject area. For example, a math team that shares all ninth- and tenth-grade students, allowing learners to "move as fast as they can, but as slow as they must" through a math curriculum that ranges from pre-algebra through trigonometry with educators specializing in various parts of the continuum. A fast-moving student might have three math teachers in a single year.

Although not yet implemented (to our knowledge), teams are considering some entirely new roles. One school is working on building a "cross-team curriculum designer" who takes the lead in designing project-based learning units for several teams at a school, shifting that complicated and time-consuming task from several individual teachers to a single and well-trained specialist. Other schools are rethinking the role of paraeducators and substitutes entirely, allowing these educators to upskill and assume roles like "Literacy Accelerators" or "Math Accelerators" where they would work with small reading, writing, or math groups.

CONCLUSION

Moving away from the "widget teacher" to a set of team-based roles that a range of educator types—from those with years of experience and proven impact to those working in other professions—can access and thrive in allows us to retain our best talent and grow the profession. The structural isolation of the normative one-teacher, one-classroom model denies educators the opportunity to interact in meaningful and sustaining ways. Team-based models, on the other hand, allow the combination of individual educator expertise to come together to form a whole that is greater than the sum of their parts.

To build educator teams, we need not look further than the current educator workforce. Most of the talent that we need already exists in the current system. It just needs to be deployed differently and informed with new mindsets and dispositions. This is important not only from a financial perspective but also when thinking about how plausible building team-based models could be. This isn't an idea that will take a generation to implement. School systems can start this work today.

The moment schools stop placing teachers in one-teacher, one-classroom models and start building teams of educators with distributed expertise, all sorts of new opportunities will emerge. Experienced and effective teachers will stay in the profession; new teachers will feel more support and stay longer; and people who left the profession to raise families may come back as part-time team members. Equally important, schools will stand a much greater chance of delivering on the promise of deepening and personalizing learning for all students.

NOTES

1. Cuban (2018).
2. Trump & Miller (1968, p. 318).
3. World Health Organization (2007).
4. World Health Organization (2007, p. 2).
5. Mdege et al. (2013).
6. Every Student Succeeds Act (2015).
7. Bureau of Labor Statistics (2022).
8. Vialet & von Moos (2020).

Chapter 3

Delivering Deeper and Personalized Learning with Teams and Technology

As students progress through our current education system with one teacher in one classroom, their engagement with school decreases. In a Gallup survey conducted in 2016, 74 percent of fifth graders reported being engaged with school, but only 32 percent of eleventh graders reported the same.[1] Early in the work of building team-based models in schools, we asked educators to help us better understand how we could better engage students. We also asked students, families, industry leaders, and community members. It was abundantly clear that all were looking for schooling to deliver something it was failing to provide.

Specifically, they wanted learning that was far more learner centered than what the system was offering. They wanted the learning to be more individualized. They wanted assessments that were relevant and addressed the problems that people grapple with every day. They wanted a much broader set of outcomes. They wanted opportunities for the student to take a larger role in driving their own learning—not just in high school—but at every level. None of this was surprising, and these sorts of approaches are well documented in the literature. But in most American schools, this sort of learning is far more likely to be the exception than the rule. Why? Because it is really, really hard to do this well—especially in the normative one-teacher, one-classroom model.

In this chapter, we want to make two big points. First, we believe students must have opportunities to learn in personalized and deep ways. Second, the only way to sustainably deliver both personalized and deep learning is to leverage teams of educators with distributed expertise who deploy technology in new and powerful ways.

OPPORTUNITIES TO LEARN IN BOTH
PERSONALIZED AND DEEP WAYS

We could spend the next several pages dissecting, debating, and differentiating the terms "personalized learning" and "deeper learning." Some might argue that these are actually the same thing—that it is impossible to have deeper learning without also personalizing that learning. Or that neither of these terms is quite right and that we should use umbrella descriptions like "student-centered learning" or "learner-centered instruction" that, ideally, contain elements of both deeper and personalized learning. Our purpose here, however, is not to sweat the taxonomy, but instead, to make this larger point: when we walk into the typical American classroom, we'd love to see students engaged in tasks that are qualitatively different from most of what we see today.

Those tasks should probably be a mixture of what we'd think of as personalized learning and deeper learning. When building Next Education Workforce models, we intentionally call out the pursuit of both personalized and deep learning because we believe that each offers important insight into what and how students should be learning.

Susan Patrick, Kathryn Kennedy, and Allison Powell define personalized learning as "tailoring learning for each student's strengths, needs and interests—including enabling student voice and choice in what, how, when and where they learn—to provide flexibility and supports to ensure mastery at the highest standards possible."[2] There is no convenient set of practices that schools can simply adopt to implement personalized learning experiences for students. Rather, delivering personalized learning requires educators to adopt and master a learner-centered way of teaching. That said, we can identify a few hallmarks of personalized learning such as individual learner profiles, customized learning paths, competency-based progressions, and flexible learning environments.

As Jal Mehta and Sarah Fine note, "Perhaps the most powerful reason to believe that deeper learning is more than a passing fad lies in the rapid and irreversible transformations to the landscape of modern life." Deeper learning, as defined by the Hewlett Foundation, includes six competencies:

- master core academic content;
- think critically and solve complex problems;
- work collaboratively;
- communicate effectively;
- learn how to learn; and
- develop academic mindsets.[3]

Ultimately, the purpose of deeper learning is to give students the tools they need to find, analyze, and apply knowledge in novel situations and contexts.[4] Students in deeper learning environments have opportunities to develop dispositions like self-direction, persistence, motivation, and curiosity. However, schools in affluent communities generally have more success in consistently providing learning experiences filled with opportunities to think critically and solve complex problems, work in collaboration with teachers and students, and demonstrate mastery of academic content and mindsets than schools in poorer communities.[5] Yet, since deeper learning experiences prepare students for college, work, civic participation, and lifelong learning,[6] we believe it should be accessible to all students, and teams help to make this possible.

Personalized learning and deeper learning, like any instructional models, are only as good as their implementations. Personalization, at its worst, conjures images of students glued to screens, with each learner moving through a bespoke playlist of activities but rarely working with others or tackling problems relevant to their own lives or the lives of others. Deeper learning, when poorly implemented, can under-deliver the critical knowledge and skills students must master to progress in higher education, succeed in the workplace, and thrive in communities. Open-ended projects turn into glorified art exhibits with high levels of ambiguity but without clear learning outcomes or academic rigor.

We have found that talking about creating opportunities for both personalized and deeper learning helps inoculate against the worst versions of these instructional approaches. Students can experience the agency and choice that comes with personalized learning while also engaging in the relevant, collaborative, and authentic tasks of deeper learning that help students build academic, self-reflective, and interpersonal dispositions and skills.

There are countless examples of individual teachers creating opportunities for both personalized and deeper learning in their classrooms. However, this work requires a level of sophistication that comes with experience, training, and support—three things that are in short supply in many under-resourced schools. We believe that every student should have access to these sorts of learning experiences and see teams of educators with distributed expertise as a sustainable and equitable way to deliver on the promise of personalized and deeper learning for all students.

THE PROMISE OF EDUCATOR TEAMS IN PERSONALIZED AND DEEPER LEARNING

When teams of educators serve a shared roster of students, they are able to use their complementary and distributed expertise to create and deliver individualized instruction, differentiated learning experiences, and multitiered supports. Moreover, deeper learning is less likely to be relegated to the single discipline of a single teacher. With teams, deeper learning can be personalized to address the perspective and interests of students.

Central to creating more opportunities for personalized and deeper learning is the ability to flexibly group and regroup students. The larger roster of students shared by an educator team, perhaps counterintuitively, creates more opportunities for strategic small groups. Group composition could be driven by student interest, proficiency in a particular skill, or complementary strengths of the students. Having more adults, who themselves have different interests, skills, strengths, and lived experiences allows for dynamic ways to support students. For example, paraeducators can support student groups who are conducting their own internet research while a professional educator with deep expertise in English Language Arts can support small groups of students with their writing. The roles that educators on the team play can—and should—look different.

To succeed in delivering deeper and personalized learning, schools should bring community educators, members of an extended team, to complement the work of a core team. Reading accelerators, or reading tutors, provide clear examples of community educators making an impact as members of teams. A reading accelerator works with students to improve their general fluency and comprehension. Whether through national programs like America Reads, local nonprofits, or parent volunteer groups, there are many ways that community educators can help personalize the experience for students.

Reading is such a clear example of the power of personalization. Conducting targeted, personalized reading instruction alone with twenty to thirty students is nearly impossible. However, a learning environment that includes a group of trained community educators allows each student to receive the personalized or small-group attention they need while allowing the professional educator(s) to work closely with students who need their attention. In all cases, not only are students getting the support they need in reading, but they are also getting opportunities to build relationships with other adults.

TECHNOLOGY-ENHANCED TEAMS TO PERSONALIZE AND DEEPEN LEARNING

When implemented well, technology plays a critical role in personalized and deeper learning. But how do we define technology? What is its proper role? And how do we best integrate it into practice? Educators have wrestled—not always successfully—with those questions for decades. Technology, however, isn't going anywhere. In fact, it has become a crucial tool as learning becomes ever more personalized and deep. The real question is this: How do we embrace technology and understand how to use it to reach more students, provide more access, and ultimately integrate it into effective teams?

Technology can play a significant role in the team both to personalize and deepen learning by helping students acquire fundamental skills and allowing them new and dynamic ways to connect with educators (and one another!) around complex and integrated ideas and content.

Technology-Enhanced Learning and New Roles

Online and artificial intelligence (AI)-enhanced programs are beginning to be developed in ways that take personalized, self-paced, competency-based learning to the next level. One of the biggest challenges we face when building team-based models is mathematics because it often plays an outsized role in sorting students into particular groups and that starts to feel a lot like tracking based on ability level.

Mathematics demands mastery of prerequisite skills in ways that other content areas typically do not. Lacking that mastery has profound implications on students' ability to understand and engage in future mathematical concepts. This problem is not new, but the solutions coming from technology-enhanced learning are new, and they are quite exciting. In fact, the most interesting Next Education Workforce models we see are those in which an educator team leverages online and AI-enhanced programs to help fill gaps in students' mathematical understanding, utilizing small-group reteaching on specific concepts for ever-changing groups of students, and also teaching on-grade-level content and collaborative, deeper, problem-based tasks with other members of the team. By using technology, teams can avoid the pitfalls of tracking and ability-level scheduling while simultaneously delivering personalized learning to individual students that support their academic advancement.

Online and AI technology not only supports personalization and deeper learning but also creates opportunities for new educator roles like lab facilitator, data analyst, or small-group tutor. As students work on self-paced, online learning, they could be supported by a lab facilitator—someone who can get students unstuck on lab tasks, keep them motivated, and communicate with the core educator team about students' progress. These people may not be professional, credentialed teachers but instead specialized paraeducators or community educators. In fact, this job description may be more analogous to an excellent youth soccer coach than to a certified professional teacher.

Technology helps to create new roles for professional educators as well. Consider the large amount of time educators spend analyzing data about student academic progress. Now, with teams, roles can be concentrated and allocated to one team member. Data feeds coming from the technology-enhanced aspects of programs spanning different content areas could be analyzed by that single individual, freeing time for other team members to work face-to-face with students in different-sized groups and individually. We can imagine how this role might be appealing to educators who love working with data and who could spend a meaningful portion of their time doing that, allowing others on the team to focus on other aspects of teaching.

Technology to Connect Students and Educators

Sadly, great educators are not universally distributed. Whether we are talking about physics teachers in rural communities or reading tutors in metropolitan centers, schools face the perpetual challenge of getting the right educators with the right students at the right time. Technology can help address this problem. Not only can it help bring new educators around students in different ways, but it can also create additional flexibility for professional educators who, for the last two centuries, have enjoyed very little flexibility in how they come to work.

Technology also opens up more possibilities to bring community educators to learners. One of the biggest challenges that schools face in integrating community educators into teams is the operational cost of showing up. Finding time to commit to working with learners is hard enough. Finding the time to drive, park, navigate the school building, and drive back home or to work is even harder. Technology helps lower the activation energy required to bring educators onto a team to support students.

Technology also gives students access to professional educators they would otherwise never see. Imagine a physics teacher who provides remote instruction to several rural schools, offering advanced content to students who would otherwise miss out on that work because the small class sizes in any one school could never justify the cost of hiring that teacher.

Additionally, teams could even consider building self-directed learning time into their schedules and allow students to pursue a wide range of topics that align with their personalized interests. Learning from an educator who doesn't work in your school isn't a new idea, but it is far more possible (and the experience is much better!) than in the past thanks to advances in technology and a growing shift in mindset around where, when, and how people learn and teach.

Finally, technology could bring much-needed flexibility into the roles of professional educators. Imagine a team with four professional educators sharing 100 students. What if each teacher on that team had the ability to work from home one day a week? Teachers could opt into this. Half of the day could be spent conferencing with individuals or small groups via technology. The other half could be spent on planning or assessment. If they needed to schedule a doctor's appointment or take care of other personal tasks, teachers could take that time off.

To some, this idea might sound outlandish. However, as Peter Cappelli of the University of Pennsylvania's Wharton School of Business describes, we must acknowledge the changing world of work and the associated tradeoffs.[7] For anyone who has ever been a teacher and needed to accomplish a task during "normal business hours," you know what we are talking about here. If we are serious about professionalizing the profession, trusting educators, and creating jobs they are interested in filling, we will need to get more creative and human centered in how we structure the jobs. Technology can help us do that.

CONCLUSION

While personalization and deeper learning can be viewed separately, we think of them as working in tandem to create richer learning experiences for students, whether they are learning fundamental skills or the deeper knowledge that requires high levels of thinking. In essence, personalized learning provides more opportunities for deeper learning.

Personalization accounts for context and individual background and experience (e.g., culturally relevant and developmentally appropriate). Deeper learning allows for application and problem solving and other skills needed to understand why students need to learn a particular topic or construct. Deeper learning can also help personalize experiences. Students can approach big questions and problems from varying perspectives so that their burgeoning interests and passions can lead them to other disciplines that they have never even heard of.

We believe that team-based staffing models are more conducive to both personalized and deeper learning than the normative one-teacher, one-classroom model. By bringing more expertise, perspective, and creativity into learning environments, team-based models are more likely to deliver deeper and more personalized learning experiences to all students. All of this will be made ever more possible thanks to meaningful and ethical advances in technology—in terms of content delivery, access to educators, and flexibility for educator teams.

NOTES

1. Gallup (2017).
2. Patrick et al. (2013).
3. Hewlett Foundation (2013).
4. Darling-Hammond et al. (2019).
5. Noguera et al. (2015).
6. Darling-Hammond et al. (2019).
7. Cappelli (2021).

Chapter 4

Entry, Specialization, and Advancement in the Next Education Workforce

In the 1980s and 1990s, much was written about the challenges schools face in attracting and retaining teachers. People concerned with the problem examined teacher career ladders, compensation systems, and the factors associated with retaining teachers through advancement. For learners, who their teachers are and how those teachers are retained are imperative. These are the people who we hope know students the best. Mobility leaves learners with no one who knows their strengths, interests, and needs from one year to the next.

Unfortunately, not much has improved. With rises in accountability, salary systems have been challenged to compensate based on student performance and levels of professional development, including attainment of advanced degrees. Roles such as teacher-on-special-assignment, department chairs, instructional coaches, or multi-classroom leaders, like those found in Opportunity Culture schools,[1] are still popular in districts.

For the most part, however, teachers do not have a lot of room to advance in the profession. Too often, advancement means moving into school administration and out of instructional roles. Indeed, there are few opportunities to advance within the learning environment—many "advanced" roles in education require educators to leave the classroom altogether. As we think about team-based staffing models, we are thinking about how people enter the profession and what they bring in terms of expertise, the kinds of specializations that allow for advancement, and other opportunities for leadership within teams—all opportunities that may keep educators in the learning environment.

As we began thinking about new kinds of roles in the Next Education Workforce, we turned to healthcare. In healthcare, there are a variety of roles and accompanying specializations. At the Mayo Clinic Hospital, there is a poster in every emergency room space that says, "Who's in My Room" (figure 4.1). It shows small squares of people who have multiple roles serving patients: registered nurses, emergency technicians, emergency physicians, respiratory therapists, laboratory technicians, pharmacy technicians, nurse's aides, and radiology technicians—all wearing different colored scrubs so you can easily know what role they play. Each has a specialization and a role to play as part of a team serving the patient's needs.

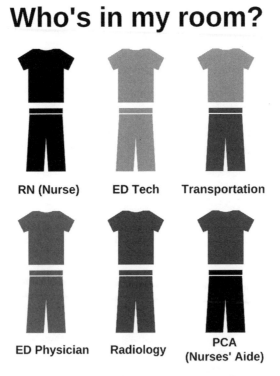

Figure 4.1   An Example of the Chart from the Mayo Hospital's Emergency Room. Showing the Various Roles of Healthcare Workers Who, as a Team, Are Meeting Patients' Needs. *Source*: Author Created.

Everyone in education who engages young learners needs to have some degree of technical knowledge and general skills. In schools, where an elementary teacher has been prepared like any other elementary teacher, there isn't the same kind of differentiation of specialization or expertise that the healthcare sector has embraced.

However, if one digs a bit deeper, one often finds that one teacher also has an endorsement in special education or second language learning. Or one finds that a secondary math teacher has extensive experience as a former engineer with expertise that is underutilized at school. So even when specialization occurs, schools just don't take advantage of it. The one-teacher, one-classroom model actually prevents educators from bringing their full skillset to the act of teaching.

We aren't suggesting that each educator should have a narrow set of specialized skills and work only in that area. What we are suggesting is that, in addition to having robust baseline knowledge and skill, professional educators should have the ability, permission, and encouragement to become specialists.

If we want to create a profession that is interesting and sustainable for educators, we must create more ways to enter the profession, more incentives to stay in the profession, and more paths to advance in the profession. This is true not only for professional educators and leaders but also for those in supporting roles as community educators and para-educators. In this chapter, we explore the better ways that educators can enter, specialize, and advance in the profession.

ENTERING THE EDUCATION FIELD

Educators currently enter the profession in many ways. They take different pathways to enter teaching at different points in their lives. Many teachers, indeed, are still in their early twenties, having recently graduated from an undergraduate teacher preparation program with a degree in elementary or secondary education. That's still the route the majority of teachers take. Others in their twenties have just graduated with a degree in a subject such as history or biology but want to enter teaching through what have been called alternative pathways.

Then there are career changers who have had experience in law, engineering, accounting, and other fields, professional and technical, who may be in residency programs—working alongside mentor teachers or in charge of classrooms of their own. Others are para-educators who have been working in schools for years and are progressing toward a degree in teaching. Paraeducators must often find a program that works with their busy schedules, both professionally and personally.

Entry for Professional Educators

There are many ways to enter the teaching profession. All of these entryways have become acceptable in most states, although they are not without concerns. The quality of teacher preparation programs varies greatly; graduates of the least effective programs, once placed in classrooms on their own, often leave within weeks. Sometimes the formats of programs are a poor fit with the real lives of students. For example, often, as paraeducators progress toward the clinical experience component of their programs, they are told they must leave their paying role in order to complete that requirement.

There are many ways to enter the profession. But education needs better ones. Schools need ways for novice teachers to join the profession not as single individuals in classrooms in hopes that they will survive and stay but as members of teams that provide professional support and opportunities for them to succeed and develop.

Team-based induction is hard to imagine in the normative one-teacher, one-classroom model. Although career changers might have an array of prior experiences, schools do not, under current norms, have the luxury of considering those experiences and how they might benefit a learning environment. Current staffing models force system and school leaders to focus merely on filling vacant positions. Too often, especially for roles that affect the most vulnerable learners, anyone who meets even the minimum criteria will do.

Even when schools have the chance to deploy educators with a variety of backgrounds in different ways, they too often deploy them as widgets—novice widgets. When individuals complete their residencies, their alternative certification pathways, or their paraeducator-to-teacher programs, they are treated as novice teachers—but they aren't the same. Not only are their entry points different, but so are their experiences, expertise, skills, and perspectives. Placing each in a classroom, alone, where only one set of students gets to take advantage (or disadvantage) no longer makes sense (if it ever did).

Entry for Community Educators

New efforts to create more career-relevant learning require people from industry and higher education. Efforts to address growing mental health and emotional concerns require expertise which the teachers may not have. Efforts to address inequitable gaps in learning require small group instruction, tutors, mentors, and so on. All cannot be done within the traditional frame. Plus, growing interest in learning initiated outside of school: community-run charter schools, pods, homeschool co-ops, and microschools tend to rely heavily on—or are run by—people with talent, but not necessarily training to work effectively with all students. This is a way to tap into new sources of talent in the community, but those folks need help to be successful.

Additionally, there are volunteers—both youth and adults—who would like to work in schools. These individuals can't—or can't make the commitment to—complete a teacher preparation program. Nor are they able to work full time in schools, perhaps because they have a different jobs. They may feel unprepared to help students in a meaningful way in the learning environment, yet they bring experiences that could immensely help to make deeper and more personalized learning experiences for students. In the current normative model, even if a volunteer comes to a school, they may only go to work in one classroom, and that one set of students in that classroom may not be the right set of students for the knowledge and experiences the volunteer has.

In Next Education Workforce models, community educators are deployed on teams and insured that they reach the right group of students for their knowledge and expertise, in and out of schools (e.g., nonprofits, neighborhoods, pods, and microschools). To do this successfully, schools should build ways for them to acquire relevant, applicable pedagogical knowledge, and skills.

This could be the work of colleges of education interested in liberating and making their content accessible to other types of educators, or the work of school districts or nonprofit organizations. If school systems or educator preparation programs could provide them with small, bite-sized, units of pedagogical knowledge, they could support learners and professional educators by supplementing instruction as content experts, content supports, or even socio-emotional supports. However, to be most beneficial, they need the right level and quality of just-in-time training.

If adequately prepared, community educators can help to deepen learning for students by working with, supporting, or building a team of novice and expert educators to design a unit of study or by teaching key parts of lessons. Community educators can also help to personalize learning for students as tutors or serve as mentors for apprenticeships. And who knows how many who dip their toe into teaching in this way might continue to become professional educators?

So, bring on better points of entry. Make it easier to support those who want to move into the field of teaching from other careers. Provide financial support and academic support for paraeducators who have never had the opportunity to finish their degree. And, bring in those who finish a degree and decide teaching is in their future, but don't put them in classrooms by themselves.

SPECIALIZING IN THE EDUCATION FIELD

At the heart of teams with distributed expertise is, in fact, expertise. We must recognize what all educators—teachers, paraeducators, and community educators—bring to the learning environment, through prior experience, in or out of schools, or knowledge gained through academic or professional learning. Staffing decisions should no longer be made just to fill slots. They must be made by looking at the needs of the learners, the requirements of the curriculum, and the areas of expertise of the educators already working in the learning environment.

Specializations for Professional Educators

Early in a teacher's preparation, they can sometimes—depending on their institution—obtain a dual certification in a single degree (e.g., elementary/special education and early childhood/English as a Second Language). Rarely does this happen at the secondary level because of content requirements without lots of preplanning on the part of the teacher candidate? And, rarely are there elective credits in any teacher preparation program. Programs are prescriptive and leave no room for voice or choice.

But what if they did? Of course, we recognize that varied certification and endorsement areas exist. Yet, what if teachers—from novice to expert—had the opportunity to specialize earlier in their professional education and practice. What if initial early career professional education didn't inevitably lead to a master's degree but, rather, provided some deeper knowledge in a subject area such as trauma-informed learning, data literacy, computer science, or problem-based learning?

Professional learning courses in such specializations could help teams broaden their expertise—their knowledge and skill sets—in a number of ways and allow both novice and experienced teachers, who might take these courses as professional learning opportunities to differentiate themselves. Such courses would allow educators to deepen their practice in ways that simultaneously meet the learning needs of their students and fuel their own professional curiosity and growth. Professional learning that leads to advanced specializations, perhaps master's degrees and other advanced professional credentials like National Board Teacher Certification, could be structured around providing educators with the skills and competencies that would strengthen their teams.

Additional professional learning may be designed for some educators who aspire to work across teams to improve the performance of schools and school systems. Systems could create new roles, such as cross-school instructional coaches who have specializations in STEM, data literacy, trauma-informed teaching and learning, and other primary needs of each team's roster of students. This cadre of specialists supporting teams of teachers in high-need areas changes the structure and system of the way schools serve the needs of students. To accomplish this, it will be essential to build specialization courses in-house or work with a local teacher preparation program provider.

Specializations for Paraeducators

It's important to recognize that paraeducators bring expertise to the learning environment. Yet, we also want to offer specializations to paraeducators and prepare them to succeed in specialized roles. This approach is common in other fields. In law, for example, paralegals are able to specialize in corporate law, estate planning, and family law. In medicine, there is a multitude of roles, like phlebotomists, medical transcriptionists, and patient care technicians that don't require medical degrees.

In education, however, paraeducators have typically been generalists. Often, they work with special education students (without the domain knowledge that specialists have) or are given tasks teachers don't want to do or simply don't have time to do. Yet, with more specialized preparation, these educators could fill specific roles on teams that meet the needs of learners. They could earn more compensation through a progression of skill building. They could have a clear path to advancement as paraeducators or, if they chose, a path to certification that would not require them to leave their job (and their students) and forego their income.

ADVANCING IN THE PROFESSION

A profession that does not offer adequate advancement opportunities can't rightly be said to be a profession at all. A healthy profession affords professionals opportunities to acquire relevant and applicable new knowledge and to take on new roles and responsibilities during the course of a career. A working environment that fails to offer educators these opportunities will fail to serve learners and will fail to retain teachers. What other profession expects that Day 1 of one's career will look like Day 3,000?

Advancement for Professional Educators

As we've already mentioned, there are few advancement opportunities for educators that allow them to take on differentiated responsibilities and earn increased compensation without having to leave the learning environment. By adopting team-based models, schools can change that. With specializations, different team members can take on new roles.

If a teacher specializes in trauma-informed learning, for example, they may be the team member responsible for ensuring students experiencing trauma get the support they need in and out of the learning environment. A teacher who specializes in data literacy may be responsible for supporting the data needs of the team. If a teacher earns advanced and specialized credentials, her responsibilities can change and, perhaps, she begins to work across several teams, meeting the specialized needs of more students and warranting higher pay.

There may also be new kinds of leadership positions—math lead, team lead, or multi-team lead or coach. Both educators and students would benefit if schools afforded educators opportunities to fulfill leadership roles and responsibilities before jumping to school leadership.

Context matters. Needs vary among schools and communities. In the Next Education Workforce models, it should be possible to align professional advancement opportunities with the needs of students.

Advancement for Paraeducators

Even someone without years of formal education, paraeducators may bring expertise in language, culture, and skills. On teams, these members are valued in ways they haven't been in the past, and with the right size training and credentialing to prepare individuals to work with students, all individuals on the team can be elevated. Typically, paraeducators do not have much room to advance. But, with new specializations, paraeducators would be able to perform differentiated roles and work across teams within a school.

To do this, they should be able to earn stackable credentials that schools recognize. And, while there has been much discussion in the field about pathways for paraeducators to become professional educators, few such pathways are systematically implemented in partnership with colleges of education.

When we reconsider how we structure teacher preparation and professional education, we should design ways to recognize the wealth of classroom experience paraeducators already have. The pursuit of additional credentials should be more accessible. Paraeducators could earn stackable credentials that translate into advancement opportunities— trainee, learning accelerator, or assistant teacher. Paraeducators should be able to conduct the clinical experience portions of any preparation program by taking on specific responsibilities on their team. This would allow them to continue earning compensation while advancing on their path to becoming a professional educator.

Advancement for Community Educators

Providing smaller roles for volunteers, tutors, and other members of the community allows a larger number of people to "try teaching on" while allowing them to perform meaningful roles that schools and learners need. We have seen many volunteers or interns, often our own college students or retirees, who enjoy working with young learners as community service. The role they play is vital, but they often do it without training or the opportunity to build and demonstrate competency toward some type of credential. The right kind of training could be beneficial and could lead more of these people into the profession.

CONCLUSION

Education must think more strategically about who's entering the profession, what skills and experience they bring, and how they can be deployed on teams that surround learners. As parents, we want them all—the new teacher from a university who brings cutting-edge practices and ideas, the experienced teacher who has specialized in an area related to the needs of the students, and the person who comes from business with applied knowledge.

We also want to keep all of these people in education. To do so, education systems need to provide clear pathways to advancement. Someone interested in teaching should have multiple entry points—as a community educator, paraprofessional, or through certification programs at the undergraduate and graduate levels. Pathways and programs should be accessible—on-demand, bite-sized learning, stackable credentials, and flexible experiences.

But multiple entry points and accessibility are not enough. Educators should be treated as professionals. Attaining specializations should increase opportunity, responsibility, and incentives. Educators should have access to the personalized professional learning and specializations they need to serve their students, and they will need to have advancement opportunities to feel like they have room to grow in ways that are valued and respected.

NOTE

1. Hassel & Hassel (2021).

Chapter 5

Approaching Equity in the Next Education Workforce

We understand that there are no easy fixes in education, especially when it comes to creating more equitable outcomes and environments for learners and teachers. Schools alone cannot overcome all of the societal and family barriers by themselves, but we must do better. It's hard to imagine doing much better than we are without finding ways to reach individual students in much more effective ways, opening up schools and classrooms to a more permeable relationship with community services and supports, and creating the conditions for people in the community, who know students' families and cultural contexts, to have a much more meaningful role in teaching.

As Next Education Workforce models are built, it will be essential to continually consider the structural and systemic equity implications of this work. To ground this work, we borrow Elena Aguilar's definition of equity:

> Every child gets what they need in our schools—every child, regardless of where they come from, what they look like, who their parents are, what their temperament is, or what they show up knowing or not knowing. Every child gets what they need every day to develop the knowledge and skills to be ready for college or a career.[1]

Equity will not be accomplished through siloed reforms to curriculum, standards, assessment, or human capital. Rather, it will take substantial structural and systemic changes. We believe that Next Education

Workforce models play a role in approaching equity by transforming the learning experiences, the roles and responsibilities of educators, how they assume those roles, and how educators work together in their roles.

APPROACHING EQUITY THROUGH TEAMS OF EDUCATORS WITH DISTRIBUTED EXPERTISE

A central premise of teams of educators with distributed expertise is that learners are now surrounded by a more diverse set of educators. These educators should be "representative of the learners, families, and communities they serve so that true culturally responsive learning is possible."[2] We posit that teams of educators can approach equity for students by creating a structure that increases the chance of a student seeing educators who represent them, their families, and their communities and by increasing learners' access to adults who can increase their social capital.

Teams of Educators Support Representation of Learners, Families, and Communities

One instance of the lack of diversity in our education workforce is seen in its national demographics. The lack of diversity among educators is of course a symptom of the many structural inequalities at work in the United States, and we ought not to pretend that the Next Education Workforce is a panacea.

While over 50 percent of K-12 students are students of color, our workforce is 79 percent white. Indeed, even in schools where the majority of students are not white, the majority of teachers tend to be white. However, there is growing evidence that a racial identity match has positive implications for student outcomes (NASEM, 2019). We acknowledge that the lack of diversity is due to the barriers to entry into the profession, which we will address later in this chapter. At hand, however, teams of educators could increase the chances that a student of color sees an educator of color. Additionally, evidence suggests that all students benefit from having an educator of color.[3]

As we continue to build Next Education Workforce models, we understand that the demographics of the workforce will not change overnight. Team members will need to build a culture that keeps each other accountable for inequitable practices, attitudes, or dispositions that negatively affect minoritized students. This cannot be the sole responsibility of one team member, especially a team member of color.

Rather, teams will need to engage in honest, trust-building, and action-oriented cogenerative dialogue that foreground educators' own personal and professional identities, how those relate to their students, and how to ethically collaborate.[4] Current educators in the field will still need to self-reflect on their own knowledge, backgrounds, and belief systems that impact their practices, which could harm students from backgrounds different from their own. When trust is present, team members can help to mitigate each other's biases.

Nevertheless, there are concrete ways Next Education Workforce models can move us toward a more diverse workforce, even if these ways require a longer time horizon as we develop pipelines and build new pathways. Often, too, our educator workforce lacks (or, as we previously mentioned, underutilizes) the diversity of industry-based experiences that many educators have.

Teams provide the opportunity for other community members to come into the classroom as community educators. These community educators, who may or may not share racial-ethnic identities with students, but may share other identities present in the local community, can help to deepen and personalize learning experiences, working as learning accelerators for reading, math, or other subjects, but can also help build students' social capital.

Teams of Educators Can Support Building Students' Social Capital

Mahnaz Charania and Julia Freedland Fisher define social capital as "students' access to, and ability to mobilize, relationships that help them further their potential and their goals," and they enumerate the many reasons why building students' social capital is "an equity imperative."[5] As we've stated in previous chapters, taking a Next Education Workforce approach to supporting students increases both the quantity and quality of those relationships students might mobilize. Not only are there more teachers in the "room" in Next Education Workforce models, but also, as we heard from a kindergarten lead teacher, taking a team-based approach allows educators to "slow down and get to know the students more."

Community educators are talented adults from the community who bring additional capacity, insight, and expertise to learning environments. In *Defining and Measuring Social Capital for Young People: A Practical Review of the Literature on Resource-full Relationships*, Peter Scales, Ashley Boat, and Kent Pekel write that

> ultimately, social capital that helps historically marginalized youth succeed within a context of systemic exclusion, racism, sexism, and discrimination has to also include "linking" social capital, which World Bank researchers . . . saw as a more "vertical" connection—resources being realized through relationships between unequals in power and domination, particularly with people in positions of authority.

By including community educators as part of a team, they have the potential to provide students with "linking" social capital.

APPROACHING EQUITY THROUGH DEEPER AND PERSONALIZED LEARNING

There is evidence that suggests that deeper and personalized learning is associated with positive outcomes for students. However, access to deeper and personalized learning opportunities has a direct connection to and implications for school staffing and structures. It's important that all students participate, no matter their skill level. It will be incumbent on the team to ensure that learners are not singled out because of their emergent skill levels that are not the same as the "norm," which often happens in traditional approaches. A team-based approach can help to broaden students' access to a variety of curricular and pedagogical approaches.

Access to deeper and personalized learning opportunities relies on access to experienced educators with truly excellent preparation relative to deeper and personalized learning approaches. High-poverty schools not only have a disproportionate percentage of less experienced teachers but also tend to employ lower-performing graduates as teachers. Students in low-income schools lack access to curriculum and learning opportunities that engage in problem-solving activities. Designing teams that have both experienced, novice teachers and others who can distribute expertise can alleviate some of these issues and provide the human capital needed to teach in deeper ways.

While the development of technology has made personalized learning more accessible, a fundamental aspect of personalized learning is the inclusion of a sentient educator who can humanize and apply learning and in so doing cultivate learner agency. Students from diverse backgrounds and with differing abilities can work both collaboratively and independently to make meaningful contributions to group tasks and to solve problems. A diverse educator workforce that includes professional teachers, paraeducators, and community educators can provide more culturally responsive and sustaining teaching that leads to more learning experiences driven by student agency to achieve personalized learning that meets the needs of each student.

Detracking the System

Society and school systems have attempted to meet the needs of individual students through tracking systems (e.g., honors versus regular versus remedial classes) based on student's ability and performance. In traditional staffing models, tracking is a structure that aims to reduce the amount and types of differentiation. In this way, tracking reduces the range of skill levels in a single class and makes the difficult job of differentiation more manageable for a single teacher. This system has historically advantaged white, gifted, and high socioeconomic students, and the system has disadvantaged students of color—black and Latino students in particular[6] and students from low socioeconomic backgrounds.[7]

Tracking in this manner has often become accepted as the norm, so much so that it is rarely questioned and may happen unintentionally through how some students are scheduled. For instance, a single honors section in a secondary schedule can create tracks for all students in that grade level.

Detracking students is a foundational component of building equitable Next Education Workforce models and providing deeper learning opportunities for all students. A team of educators working together can better meet the needs of individual learners. Teams can evaluate student needs and group learners flexibly over time. Rather than tracking, teams of educators can work with students to develop personalized learner profiles that utilize multiple streams of data, including nonacademic data such as student interests.[8] These personalized profiles might also include detail about pedagogical approaches that work best for students. The co-construction of learner profiles can inform educators' culturally responsive teaching practices that integrate multiple opportunities for students to have agency over their learning experiences.

APPROACHING EQUITY THROUGH NEW AND BETTER ENTRY, SPECIALIZATION, AND ADVANCEMENT PATHWAYS

We need lower-risk opportunities for prospective educators to test the profession. One way to do this might be to create new roles with lower barriers to entry (either in terms of time or cost). This might, in turn, increase the opportunity for a more diverse group of people to determine if a professional pathway is right for them before committing to a formal degree or preparation program. When possible, these new roles should also have hourly wages, and any preparation for them should ideally count toward a larger credential. These roles could be made available to a wide range of people, including high school students, parents, and potential career switchers.

Paid residency opportunities in teacher-preparation programs might be another way to increase diversity. Evidence suggests that "support and assistance for beginning teachers have a positive impact on three sets of outcomes: teacher commitment and retention, teacher classroom instructional practices, and student achievement."[9] New teachers with more training in teaching methods and pedagogy are far more likely to remain in the classroom after their first year on the job.[10] We also know that a growing number of educators enter through pathways that require less preservice preparation and that educators entering through those pathways are disproportionately teachers of color.[11]

Higher-quality preservice training options often levy significant opportunity costs on participants. A full-time, nonpaying residency program often means that the person cannot have a job or has to maintain a paying job on top of an already full schedule. The highest-quality preservice options are therefore biased toward those future educators who have the luxury of not needing to earn income while conducting a residency. Having a paid residency program would help to level that playing field, making the highest-quality preparation paths more accessible to those from lower-income backgrounds.

Advancement and Specializations in the Profession

Advancement pathways built around competencies, not seat time, would value an educator's experience without lowering the expectations for the knowledge, skills, and dispositions required to be successful in specific roles. Having raised a family or worked for years as a classroom aide should translate into competencies that education systems value. Given that there are nearly 1.3 million teaching assistants in the United States[12] and that, on average, these educators tend to be disproportionately educators of color, creating more equitable ways for those who want to advance in the profession should be a priority. We should create human capital management systems that value experience and that actively seek to diversify the education workforce—and not just in lower-paying positions, but across the entire spectrum of educator roles (and care must be taken to ensure that is true).

As mentioned earlier, educators of color disproportionately enter the profession through less robust preservice pathways (e.g., alternative certification), and data suggest that educators entering through those pathways are more likely to leave the profession.[13] Ultimately, creating more opportunities for educators of color to enter through higher-quality preservice pathways would be best.

Until then, it would stand to reason that providing more sheltered induction to the profession would benefit all educators and especially those who entered through less robust pathways. In this way, newly minted teachers would be responsible for the parts of the job where they would be successful and allow them to take on more responsibilities over time. Team-based models, where first-year teachers share rosters of students with more experienced educators could help provide both mentorship and sheltered, right-sized roles for new teachers.

Team-based models may also help address the top reasons why educators of color leave the profession at higher rates than white educators. While the number of educators of color entering the profession has increased over time, they leave the profession at rates that are 20 percent higher than their white colleagues.[14] The reasons for their departure are manifold, but topping the list is job satisfaction and, specifically, the way schools are administered, how students are assessed, a lack of input in decision-making, and a lack of autonomy over their teaching.[15] All of these factors associated with disproportionate rates of educators of color leaving their placements, in some way, may be ameliorated in Next Education Workforce models.

While it is too early to tell if Next Education Workforce models can help schools increase retention among educators of color, the models are at least designed to address the reasons educators of color self-report for leaving their placements. By providing greater autonomy at the team level and by committing to instructional models that promote deeper and personalized learning, schools could potentially address issues of administration, student assessment, and decision-making by shifting greater levels of autonomy to the team level. Restructuring and lowering the cost of advanced credentials may help open advancement pathways for educators from a wider range of backgrounds.

Most current systems of professional advancement reward degree attainment, usually in the form of master's and doctoral degrees. Requiring an advanced degree for professional advancement imposes an unnecessarily high barrier to completion because of the extensive time demands and high out-of-pocket costs. The cost of a master's degree in education at an in-state public university, for example, is about $13,000.[16] The cost of tuition may limit the number of educators who can pursue advancement, and it almost certainly limits the access of educators from lower socioeconomic backgrounds.

Imagine a different advancement system in which educators could attain specializations smaller than advanced degrees that confer additional financial benefit. Specializations could be offered at a lower price point and take less time to complete, thereby providing access for a greater number of educators. The specializations could be stacked toward an advanced degree, providing flexibility for educators to determine their timelines for degree attainment, should they pursue that path. Stacking specializations would allow educators to receive the financial benefit of incremental pay increases over time while simultaneously pacing their financial investment and providing flexibility for completion.

With a broader range of educators gaining access to advancement pathways, and with educator teams that need team members with specialization, more opportunities will be available for meaningful use of specializations such as culturally sustaining pedagogy, trauma-informed instruction, and restorative justice practices.

Leadership

Most opportunities for leadership in the current educator workforce are limited to district- and school-level administration or grade-level or department leadership. The former set of leadership opportunities are relatively few and often require significant investments of both time and money. The latter are middle-level leadership positions that have little power to drive change and rely on support from both administration and teachers who they often do not manage or supervise.[17] Next Education Workforce models create the potential for a team-based leadership position (e.g., lead teacher), a role that would not only be associated with increased compensation but would also have far more autonomy and responsibility for the success of the team and the students that team serves.

CONCLUSION

We don't believe that the Next Education Workforce will eliminate the vast inequities that plague our educational system, but we do believe that these models can significantly diminish inequality with more targeted supports; add checks and balances of more than one adult to one classroom; increase the ability to implement the kinds of complex instruction that require teacher autonomy to implement personalized and deep learning; and change hiring, evaluation, and other human resources systems that have been standing in the way.

We can wait no longer to offer an alternative to the system that systematically denies low income and students of color access to great educators and rigorous and relevant learning experiences. We can no longer sit idly by as the system systematically fails to recognize the assets of our communities and creates hurdles for low-income educators and educators of color to access training and advancement opportunities reserved for those who have more money and time. As we design and build the Next Education Workforce, we know we are hypothesizing the benefits; we are also proceeding with caution and eyes wide open. We know that we will need to continually reflect on these inequities, keep them at the forefront of our work, and act in a way that ensures that this system ameliorates inequities—not compounds them.

NOTES

1. Aguliar (2013, para. 3).
2. AASA (2021, p. 8).
3. Carver-Thomas (2018).
4. Boveda & Weinberg (2020).
5. Charania & Fisher (2020).
6. McCardle (2020).
7. Batruch et al. (2018).
8. Pane et al. (2015).
9. Ingersoll & Strong (2011).
10. Ingersoll et al. (2014).
11. Carver-Thomas (2018).
12. Bureau of Labor Statistics, U.S. Department of Labor (2022).
13. Redding & Smith (2016).
14. Ingersoll et al. (2017).
15. Ingersoll et al. (2017).
16. Arizona State University (n.d.).
17. Darling-Hammond (2001).

Chapter 6

The Next Education Workforce in Three School Models

Trogon Elementary, Quail High School, and Redstart K-8

This chapter provides us with three examples of what schools might look like as they become Next Education Workforce schools. None of these schools are real; however, each reflects aspects of schools with whom we have been lucky enough to partner. These representative schools model the elements purported to be in place to create the kind of learning and working environments that are conducive for educators and students: teams of educators with distributed expertise; commitment to deeper and personalized learning; and better ways to enter, specialize, and advance in the profession.

SCHOOL PROFILE: TROGON ELEMENTARY

Demetrio Olmos is the principal of Trogon Elementary School, a K-6 school with around 500 students. When Principal Olmos joined Trogon, his teachers were deployed in one-teacher, one-classroom models like figure 6.1.

Principal Olmos is taking steps to employ the design elements of the Next Education Workforce. He believes that it will deliver better learning experiences for his students and better working conditions for his teachers. Principal Olmos wants to do the following:

- Create cross-grade level teams with shared rosters in grades K-1, 2-3, and 4-6

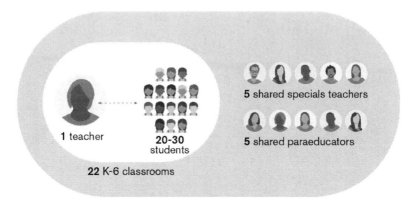

Figure 6.1 The One-Teacher, One-Classroom Model at Trogon Elementary. *Source*: Author Created.

- Support the development of shared, cross-curricular materials
- Increase SEL support, create opportunities for educators to increase the distribution of expertise, and create opportunities for role advancement that keep educators in the learning environment and allow them to specialize.

Teams of Educators

Principal Olmos has created cross-grade level teams for his K-1, 2-3, and 4-6 (figure 6.2). Now, rather than having only one set of twenty-five students, educators share groups of about eighty students and are able to utilize their distributed expertise to deliver learning experiences to students.

Learning Space

Trogon Elementary had the opportunity to redesign learning spaces to make them flexible and responsive to student needs and groupings. Pictured in figure 6.3 is the learning space, including a STEM Lab where students can design, build, and work on interdisciplinary projects. The doors between classrooms also allow educators to collaborate in real time and make adjustments to instruction accordingly. While the classrooms are labeled by subject area, it is possible that students could be learning mathematics, for example, in all learning spaces at the same time.

Teams in K-1 and 2-3

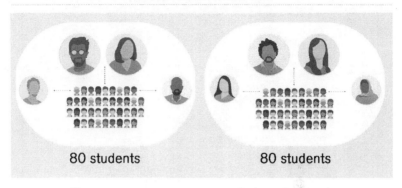

80 students   80 students

Two teams comprising two certified teachers and
two residents for each of Grades K-1 and 2-3.

Teams in 4-6

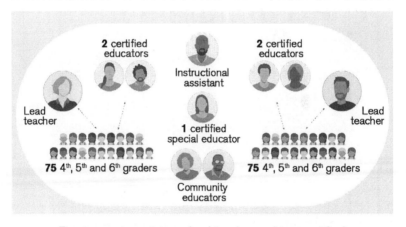

Two teams comprising a lead teacher and two certified
teachers across Grades 4-6. A certified SLD teacher,
a paraeducator, and two community educators support
both teams.

Figure 6.2   Vertical Teams at Trogon Elementary. *Source*: Author Created.

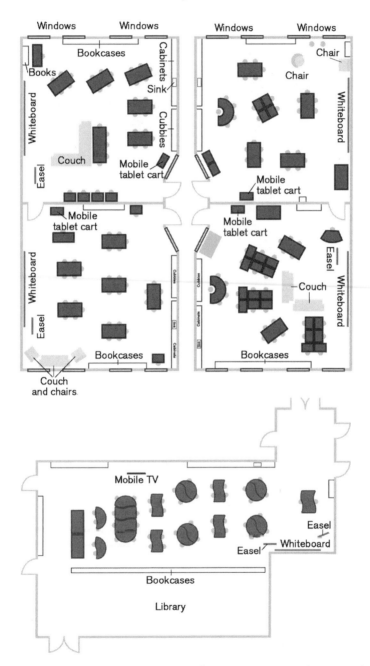

Figure 6.3   The Learning Space at Trogon Elementary. *Source*: Author Created.

Deeper and Personalized Learning

Building teams at Trogon now allows educators to better deliver deeper and personalized learning experiences to students. Students are able to build learner agency during Genius Hour, work on interdisciplinary project-based tasks, and receive personalized reading intervention. Principal Olmos has redesigned the schedule to ensure that deeper and personalized learning is possible.

Genius Hour

During Genius Hour, students build their agency in their own learning by brainstorming, researching, and presenting topics and their findings to their peers and educators. Students construct their own timelines for their projects and topics. A student may engage with a topic for a couple of days or over several weeks. Educators find ways to connect topics students are exploring in their core content classes, such as plants, and empower them to share when their topic is relevant. This time allows students to personalize their deeper learning experiences.

Project-Based Learning

The 4-6 Grade Team planned a nine-week, interdisciplinary unit on building playgrounds. This team wanted an engineer to serve as a project-based mentor for an hour a week during the unit. While they found willing individuals, the engineers could not commit to the travel time needed to meet at Trogon's campus each week. At first, this seemed like a massive operational challenge. However, with video-based conferencing, the engineer was able to meet with the students each week, right from her desk. Knowing that face-to-face interaction would only make these sorts of engagements better, the engineer prioritized coming to the school during weeks one and nine. A hybrid model in which the engineer came in person for two weeks and videoconferenced for the other seven weeks made this possible for the engineer.

Personalized Reading Intervention

During daily reading intervention time for the 2-3 Grade Team, students work in small groups and receive individualized learning experiences based on data collected throughout the week. Each Friday, educators have time to analyze the data to best determine how to group students for the upcoming week, and which groups of students will work with which educator, based on the educator's expertise. As students progress, they move between groups when necessary. During this time, the special educator also joins the team to provide specialized support. Finally, to further personalize learning, college students and a retired educator, serving as community educators, meet with the same small reading group once a week as part of a community service course.

Scheduling

Principal Olmos knows that educator teams need ample planning time to meet the needs of Trogon's students. On Fridays of each week, student groups attend a weekly project-based learning block. This time is led by the librarian and media specialist teachers, who are supported by special teachers, paraeducators, and community educators. During this time, the core team has collaborative planning time.

- Monday–Thursday: teacher-led instruction.
- Friday: project-based learning blocks (2.5 hours per grade band for students; educator teams collaborate and plan).

Specialization and Advancement Pathways

Initially, Principal Olmos only created a lead teacher role for the 4-6 educator team. Now, he is considering adding similar roles to the K-1 and 2-3 teams, too. This lead teacher still works directly with students but is also charged with leading the team in curriculum design and helping to determine how to deploy the educators.

Each educator is able to develop professional expertise in a specific content area, such as mathematics, or another specialization, such as trauma-informed education. These specializations are determined by the interests and strengths of the individual educators, by the needs of the students, and by the needs of the team.

All community educators have completed an on-demand, virtual course sequence to introduce them to their roles and responsibilities. These nano-courses, each about ten minutes in length, were created by the district in collaboration with a local college. These community educators—who include college students, a retired educator, and an engineer—come into the learning environment to deepen and personalize learning for students.

SCHOOL PROFILE: QUAIL HIGH SCHOOL

Quail High School is a large, comprehensive high school. Tish Okpara is the principal. When Principal Okpara arrived at Quail, the school's approach to staffing was a one-teacher, one-classroom model. Various subjects had different levels of enrollment.

Upon reviewing data, Principal Okpara recognized that failure rates were highest in ninth grade—students' first year at Quail. As a result, she is employing elements of Next Education Workforce models, which, at the secondary level, require changes to scheduling. Depending on the success of the ninth-grade team-based model, Principal Okpara will scale to the entire school in the future. For the ninth graders at Quail, the school is implementing the following:

- Ninth-grade educator teams with distributed expertise who share a common roster of students, in addition to new roles and responsibilities for some educators that keep them in the learning environment (e.g., lead teacher)
- Blocks of time for deeper, interdisciplinary, and inquiry-based projects for students
- Increased socio-emotional learning supports for students.

Teams of Educators

Principal Okpara has built 8 educator teams that each serve 150 students. Each team has a core educator team and an extended educator team composed of multiple educators.

Core Team

Each core team has one lead teacher and three professional educators. The teams are staffed by educators who are passionate about a specific career area such as arts, sustainability, sports and wellness, health professions, coding, entrepreneurship, agriculture, and legal studies, including a career and technical education (CTE) teacher (see figure 6.4). Each core team looks like a variation of figure 6.5 but teams are composed of educators depending on the composition of the group of students the educators are serving. Some educators (e.g., special educators) are shared across teams.

Extended Team

Each core team is also supported by an extended team. The extended team is composed of foreign language teachers, music teachers, visual and performing arts teachers, and community educators. The community educators work with the CTE teachers to deepen and personalized learning, based on the team's career focus. Figure 6.5 depicts this.

Learning Space

The learning space (see figure 6.6) is designed for flexibility. Three classrooms are separated by collapsible room dividers. This allows the educator team to think dynamically about their space and schedule. Often, two or three classrooms merge together for extended periods of time so that educators can co-teach interdisciplinary lessons.

The space also allows educators to collaborate with one another in real time. For example, as students on one topic team explored a cross-curricular unit, the educators are able to retract the walls and roam around the entire learning space to help students and converse with other educators. When learning spaces with retractable walls are not available, teams have utilized gymnasium space, auditorium

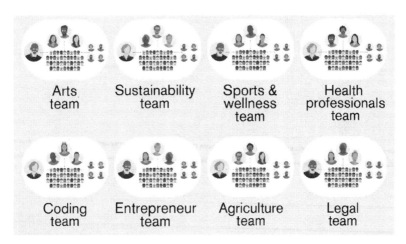

Figure 6.4   Ninth-Grade Teams at Quail High School. *Source*: Author Created.

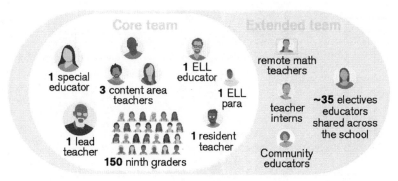

Figure 6.5 An Example of a Core and Extended Team at Quail High School. *Source: Author Created.*

and amphitheater, football fields, and other large areas for large-group time.

Deeper and Personalized Learning

Building teams at Quail now allows educators to deliver deeper and personalized learning experiences to students. The core teams prioritize making cross-curricular connections among English, math, science, and their team's topic of study. Teams utilize technology to deepen and personalize learning by using adaptive software. Additionally, students are able to guide their learning during specified inquiry- and project-based times. Career experts, both the CTE teachers and community educators, assist during inquiry- and project-based times, in addition to others, to deepen learning for students and connect their learning to knowledge and skills that will be applicable in the workforce.

Technology in Deeper and Personalized Learning

Quail has adopted an adaptive learning software for mathematics, a platform to engage students in analyzing information and creating solutions for English and social studies, and a learning management system for all content. For more systematized credit recovery—as many students need credit recovery in science—Quail employs distance-learning courses, some of which are created by their district and others of which are purchased from educational technology companies. This technology

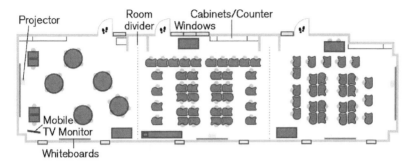

Figure 6.6 The Learning Space at Quail High School. *Source*: Author Created.

enables educators to have instant data about student learning so teachers can intervene in real time while also giving students flexibility in how and when they engage with their content.

Inquiry- and Project-Based Learning

Quail ninth graders have the opportunity to explore topics related to their own interests and work on projects to demonstrate their learning. These blocks are scheduled into their day and help students to build agency and autonomy in their learning.

Career Teams and Deeper Learning

Each team has an identity associated with a career-related field and those identities help focus the pursuit of deeper learning. For example, the Agricultural Team at Quail high school works closely with the agricultural CTE program. This provides them with hands-on and in-depth experiences working on an actual farm, as Quail has a working farm with vegetable gardens and livestock like chickens, pigs, cows, and emus. Two days a week, students learn how to grow vegetables, tend to laying hens, and learn sustainable practices.

While not all the students on the Agricultural Team go on to pursue the agricultural CTE pathway later in their high school careers, all students benefit from this experience. This now becomes an added curricular element. Students can connect their complex biology content in authentic ways, from mathematical thinking to tending to the vegetables, and writing to discuss sustainable practices.

Scheduling

Principal Okpara knows that collaborative planning time will be essential. Daily, educators have co-planning time while their students go to their electives. Students either go to their electives in the morning (providing co-planning time for the educator team in the morning)—split one in the morning, lunch, and afternoon (providing co-planning time for the educator team during this split)—or in the afternoon (providing co-planning time for the educator team in the afternoon). Student-centered instruction blocks allow for the educator team to adjust the schedule to student needs.

For instance, the English teacher may need more time to work with students on narrative writing on Tuesday, so the math and biology teachers adjust their instruction based on the remaining time in the block. Or, if the math teacher and biology teacher want to teach an interdisciplinary lesson together, they can have a longer block to ensure they teach the entire lesson. You can see this in figure 6.7.

Stacking Teaching Time

Monday	Tuesday	Wednesday	Thursday	Friday	
		Morning Meeting			
Inquiry/ Project-based learning	Student-centered (i.e., math, ELA, biology)	Student-centered content (i.e., math, ELA, biology)	Student-centered content (i.e., math, ELA, biology)	Inquiry/ Project-based learning	Students work in their Arts or Sustainability teams
		Inquiry/ Project-based learning			
		Lunch and tutoring			
Students: Elective A Educators: Co-planning time					Students attend electives while the teachers in the Arts and Sustainability teams co-plan
Students: Elective B Educators: Co-planning time					

Figure 6.7 **The Schedule at Quail High School.** *Source*: Author Created.

Specialization and Advancement Pathways

With input from her educators, Principal Okpara has decided that one teacher from each team will serve as the lead teacher for that team. These lead teachers facilitate team meetings, support other team members while they plan for instruction, provide coaching and mentorship, and act as a bridge between school administration and the team. Educators on the team have the ability to specialize and work across teams as specialists in deeper learning, personalized learning, and more.

Community educators come and help deepen and personalize learning during project- and inquiry-based learning blocks. The school is beginning to play with week-long intercessions three times a year. During these breaks, representatives from the municipality, local industry, a local university, and nonprofit organizations will teach week-long mini-courses to the ninth graders, overseen by school administration and district coaches. The core educator teams will use this protected time to plan upcoming interdisciplinary units and pursue personalized professional learning in areas the team has identified as relevant to student needs.

SCHOOL PROFILE: REDSTART K-8 SCHOOL

Redstart K-8 School is a rural school with 180 students (~20 per grade level), most of whom speak Spanish and English. Sofia Lopez is the principal. In the past, Redstart has staffed using a traditional one-teacher, one-classroom model for grades K-5 and departmentalized by subject in grades 6-8. Like many rural schools, Redstart faces struggles to find qualified teachers each year. Often, Principal Lopez has to hire an uncredentialed individual to cover for a grade level or she resorts to combining grade levels where one teacher is responsible for delivering two grade levels worth of content to up to forty students. Notably, this happens the most in her upper grades—sixth through eighth—where the content knowledge becomes more complex.

Principal Lopez and her faculty, with district support, want to utilize the design elements of the Next Education Workforce to reinvent Redstart. She believes that it will not only help with her frequent staffing shortages but also deliver more meaningful learning experiences to Redstart's students. Principal Lopez is:

- creating cross-grade-level teams who share rosters of students in grades 1-2, 3-4-5, and 6-7-8.
- utilizing technology to bring in a remote teacher for 6-7-8 math and a community educator, a local community college student who is studying to be a math teacher, as a "lab facilitator" for math.
- bringing in a community educator, a parent, who is fluent in Spanish, to facilitate project-based learning experiences in Spanish.

Teams of Educators

Principal Lopez has created three, cross-grade level teams: 1-2, 3-4-5, and 6-7-8 grades. The core team for each cross-grade level team is composed of two to three professional educators. In 6-7-8, the lab facilitator is part of the core team. The extended team is composed of the project-based learning facilitator, the art teacher, and the PE teacher.

Cross-Grade-Level Teams

After reviewing Redstart's data, Principal Lopez recognizes that students are at varying levels of proficiency across the content areas. Sometimes, for example, students are above grade level in math but below grade level in English. By creating multi-grade teams, Principal Lopez provides the opportunity for the educators to group and regroup students as the data continues to suggest. Principal Lopez has opted not to put her kindergarten class in a cross-grade-level environment; there's no local preschool, this is the first time many of these children have been in a school environment, and she wants to focus on socialization with these students.

A Lab Facilitator for 6-7-8 Mathematics

Principal Lopez hired a remote teacher to teach 6-7-8 math at Redstart. The students, however, will need supervision. She has hired a local community college student, Sebastian, who is studying to be a math teacher, as a community educator to serve as a lab facilitator for the 6-7-8 math classes. His job is to keep students engaged, making progress toward their goals, and will serve as the primary point of contact with the remote teacher.

A Spanish-Speaking Community Educator

Since many of the students at Redstart already speak Spanish, Principal Lopez has decided to hire a parent, Maria, who wants to have the same schedule as her child, to come and enrich during Genius Hour. Maria majored in Chicano/a Studies at a university and she comes in every Wednesday to help students with inquiry-based projects.

Learning Space

Redstart's learning space has not physically changed; however, students and educators view multiple classrooms as their learning space. Daily, the students on the 1-2 team meet in the cafeteria for morning meeting and then return to a pair of classrooms that they move between throughout the day. The students in the 3-4-5 team meet in the gym daily for their morning meeting and, similarly, move between three classrooms throughout the day. All teams are able to use either of the larger spaces when they are working on whole team projects, and Principal Lopez helps to coordinate this.

Deeper and Personalized Learning

Building teams at Redstart has helped to provide deeper and personalized learning experiences for students. Students have a Genius Hour which has a Spanish-speaking community educator to deepen learning experiences. Math for grades 6, 7, and 8 is personalized with the help of adaptive software. A quarter-based schedule allows students to rotate through elective courses.

Genius Hour with a Spanish Speaker

On Wednesdays, a community educator comes in to support Genius Hour experiences in Spanish. She helps students to explore the Spanish language and Hispanic culture through inquiry-based learning. Students who are not proficient in Spanish spend a portion of this time on an online language learning software which personalizes their learning but still have the opportunity to explore culture, history, art, and more.

Personalizing Learning in 6-7-8 Math

In addition to the remote math teacher, students use an online, adaptive math software application that targets gaps in their mathematical knowledge and skills. Their lab facilitator, who is training to be a math teacher, is also able to help students when necessary.

Scheduling

Students have a daily hour for electives. For two quarters, students attend PE, music/art on Monday, Tuesday, Thursday, and Friday and switch in the second quarter, and the library every Wednesday. During specials time, this becomes co-planning time for the core educator team.

Specialization and Advancement Pathways

Advancement for Sebastian, the Lab Facilitator

As a community educator, Sebastian is a paid member of the core educator team. He graduated from the local high school, where he participated in the school's grow-your-own Teacher Academy. Sebastian has always had astute ability in math and secured a scholarship to the local community college because of his stellar high school GPA. Once finished at the community college, he will not have to move to finish his teacher preparation program. Instead, he will be able to continue to work as a lab facilitator at Redstart because the state's teacher preparation program provider has a distance-learning option. As part of his grow-your-own program, he was offered a conditional teaching contract. Once he finishes his teacher preparation program, he will be able to smoothly transition into the role of math teacher for 6-7-8 at Redstart.

Specialization for Multilingual and Multicultural Education

Because a majority of students speak Spanish, Principal Lopez has worked with one of the state's universities to develop a specialization for educators who work with multilingual students to deliver a multicultural education (about nine credit hours, composed of nine one-credit courses). She is working with the university to inform the creation of other specializations, including trauma-informed education, deeper learning, personalized learning, and more. Working with her district's director of HR, Ms. Lopez plans to recognize each specialization that a teacher earns with a $500 increase in base salary.

Table 6.1 The Schedule at Redstart K-8

	K	1-2	3-4-5	6-7-8
7:00 a.m.–7:45 a.m.	Breakfast	Breakfast	Breakfast	Breakfast
7:45 a.m.–8:00 a.m.	Morning Meeting	Morning Meeting	Morning Meeting	Morning Meeting
8:00 a.m.–9:00 a.m.	Content Block 1	Specwial	Content Block 1	Genius Hour
9:00 a.m.–10:00 a.m.		Genius Hour		Specials
10:00 a.m.–11:00 a.m.	Content Block 2	Content Block 1	Genius Hour	Content Block 1
11:00 a.m.–12:00 p.m.	Lunch/Recess	Lunch/Recess	Lunch/Recess	
12:00 p.m.–1:00 p.m.	Content Block 2	Content Block 1	Special	Lunch/Recess
1:00 p.m.–2:00 p.m.	Genius Hour	Content Block 2	Content Block 2	Content Block 2

CONCLUSION

Context matters when building Next Education Workforce models. What is common about all of these representative models is that they are employing the design elements of the Next Education Workforce. These schools are providing opportunities for teachers to team, providing protected time to collaborate, and intentionally designing deeper and personalized learning experiences. They are leveraging various human capital resources, such as the community and local teacher preparation programs, to bring more adults around students. Finally, there are clear ways to enter, specialize, and advance in the profession in each model.

Part II

CONDITIONS TO LAUNCH AND SUSTAIN THE NEXT EDUCATION WORKFORCE

Chapter 7

School Leadership and Readiness for Change

Having worked with dozens of schools that have transitioned from one-teacher, one-classroom staffing models to teams with distributed expertise (and, perhaps more importantly, several schools that haven't), we've come to realize that the single biggest factor in successfully navigating that change is the building-level leader.

Principals face challenging working conditions and stressful accountability systems. It's no surprise that turnover among school leaders is high. One 2017 study found that around 18 percent of principals had left their position the previous year. In higher-poverty schools, the rate was 21 percent.[1] Such leadership turnover means drastic losses in specific institutional and community knowledge, as well as general leadership skills.

The work of redesigning schools and school systems requires strong, committed leadership. As we've said before, this work moves at the speed of trust. District and school leaders need to be responsive and agile to teachers, learners, and parents as schools navigate uncertainty. This is no small task. They need to guide the development of new organizational structures, have open communication with families and other stakeholders, and work to craft and enact a vision of how students can learn in deeper and more personalized ways. They need to deeply understand how teams function, how expertise is distributed, and how to build those processes efficiently to ensure a high level of instruction. All of these demands ask more of school leaders than the normative one-teacher, one-classroom model does. It asks them to be learning systems and learner-centered leaders.

Learner-centered leaders think first about the learners. They don't just distribute groups of students to widget teachers. Learner-centered leaders think about groups of learners and then think about the right kinds of systems to build around them. When building leaders move their focus from instruction to the learner, they can begin to frame the systems of schools around learners and learning—not framing them as ways to just get learners through the system. Learning systems leadership focuses on all the systems of a school (e.g., space, logistics, technology, staffing, assessment, and evaluation). Learning systems leadership is about more than just managing a school. It's about designing and building a learning environment.

Learning systems leaders surround themselves with others who push their thinking, bring varying perspectives to the table, and aren't afraid to take risks and share ideas. Schools must have leadership that is flexible and nimble, always maintaining a grand vision to meet the challenges and demands of both their staff and their learners. To accomplish this, leaders need building-level teams and need to be part of a team. They must find the people who are ready to get on board and let them go, give them time to succeed and fail, and guide and follow their lead simultaneously.

Today, school leaders don't have an organizational structure that is conducive to delegation or shared decision-making. Schools that implement team-based models can provide leaders with a trusted group of team leads, specialists, and operations staff who, collectively, meet a school's instructional and operational needs.

THE NEXT EDUCATION WORKFORCE LEADER

As in any organizational transformation, leadership is pivotal. Next Education Workforce leaders will need to be prepared to lead systems-level solutions. We posit they will need four things: (1) a principled mindset for decision-making; (2) the imagination to envision a different kind of schooling than what they, and most others, have experienced; (3) the ability to be learner-centered; and (4) the will to distribute leadership.

A Principled Mindset for Decision-Making

Effective leadership requires the "ability to imagine new concepts, catalyze ideas, and form new solutions that create positive change for humanity."[2] Leaders trying to catalyze transformational change should ask themselves, when they reach crucial decision points, "We can, but should we?" Educators make thousands of decisions everyday, usually expeditiously and by themselves. Those decisions impact the lives of millions of people—children, families, and communities. It's critical that educators ask the right questions at the right time but with the support of a team of leaders who can think carefully and critically.

It's vital that decisions are driven by intellectual, moral, civic, and performance assets. Intellectual decision-making enables individuals to become systems-thinkers who are innovative, creative, and engage in critical and compassionate reflection. Moral decision-making supports decisions from multiple perspectives allowing one to honestly evaluate situations with open-mindedness, integrity, equity, and justice in order to respond in a meaningful and responsible manner.

Civic-minded decision-making is a commitment to the public good. Performance-focused decision-making enables leaders to navigate uncertainty, anticipate and mitigate intended and unintended consequences, and work collaboratively to design and implement creative and effective solutions. When school leaders are not isolated and develop this mindset for decision-making with a team of their own, they model for their teams of educators a culture that also supports learners in ways that mitigate bias, decrease unintended consequences, and increase equitable outcomes.

Imagination

Leaders and leadership training talk about vision all the time, but real vision takes imagination. It is the ability to envision something new, and completely different that addresses the goals you want to achieve for both educators and learners. This is what people do when they invent, discover, and take old things to new levels. An imaginative leader must question long-held assumptions about "normal" educational structures (e.g., common bell schedules) and practices (e.g., hiring substitutes) and, when appropriate, bravely do things differently. They must share the belief that all learners and educators can excel, that the learning environment can be personalized, and that deeper learning can and should occur. Having imagination and allowing others to imagine with you can lead to new ways of thinking, doing, and learning.

Distributed Leadership

The old saying "it's lonely at the top" couldn't be more true in schools. Team-based models provide opportunities for multiple leaders—like team leads—to exist and collaborate. Distributed leadership is, "First and foremost about leadership practice rather than leaders or their roles, functions, routines, and structures."[3] In this case, the relationship and interaction among school leaders in Next Education Workforce models open opportunities for school leaders not only to have an assistant principal but also to have a real leadership team.

This is a team that guides strategy, watches closely how teams function, pays close attention to individual and collective data to ensure that no learner is falling through the cracks, and works quickly to remove obstacles, especially anything that looks like, "we've always done it this way." While educators are focused on distributing expertise on their teams, leaders will need to know how to build teams, how to train team leads, and how to distribute leadership to those team leads as well as other specialists. Educators' interdependence is paramount to their successful operation, and, by extension, the successful execution of learning experiences for students.

Readiness for Change

To be ready for the Next Education Workforce, a leader must have in place the following:

- *Culture of collaboration*: A culture of collaboration, built on mutual trust and respect, exists among students, educators, staff, and administration.
- *Thoughtful change management*: Organizational culture and processes exist to support the move to new models of teaching, learning, and staffing.
- *Supportive leadership*: Innovative leaders at the school and district levels are willing to test new ideas and empower teams to improve outcomes for students and educators.
- *Transparency*: All stakeholders, and especially students and families, have unobstructed views into changes being made and have frequent, authentic opportunities to provide a voice in decision-making.

Any change is challenging. Moving away from the normative one-teacher, one-classroom model of schooling is very hard. As school leaders assess the readiness of their schools or systems to implement Next Education Workforce models, they need to think carefully about change, moving at the speed of trust, usually with one team that may raise their hand and say, "We are ready!" Leaders who have made the commitment to team-based models say things like, "I'd never go back to staffing schools with one teacher in one classroom."

They also say that the work is challenging and that, especially at the start, leaders must continue to hold the vision or else the normative forces will pull educators back into the siloed roles that have dominated staffing models for decades. While this seems complex, we believe there are leaders and educators and, certainly, parents and students ready for something radically different.

CONCLUSION

Many teachers say that each year's group of students is unique and has different needs. They talk about the general makeup of the class, gender, special needs, and language acquisition needs. All these things that teachers observe are signals, not noise. They are data points that should contribute to how leaders design teams to meet the needs of students. And meeting the learning needs of students by deploying the right mix of expertise among educators is the kind of systems leadership for which school leaders should be held accountable.

We are seeing glimpses of this in microschools, teacher-led pods within districts, and schools that share teachers across schools. Leadership can no longer be only about instructional practice or instructional leadership; it has to be about configuring human capital in more effective ways, forming the right teams around learners, and providing learner and educator agency through distributed leadership.

NOTES

1. Goldring & Taie (2018).
2. Mary Lou Fulton Teachers College, Arizona State University (2019, p. 4).
3. Spillane (2005).

Chapter 8

Transforming Teacher Preparation and Professional Learning for Teams

As we've stated, teaming is not new. But we have to ask ourselves: Why didn't teaming stick? We believe that one of the key reasons is that neither teacher preparation nor in-service professional development changed to support team-based models. Throwing preservice and in-service teachers into teams without proper training isn't going to work any more than throwing them into open classrooms, asking them to teach math with manipulatives, or requiring them to implement a new curriculum—without preservice preparation and professional learning that is designed for the work we are asking educators to perform. Learning how to be a strong team member, focused on the mission of the organization, student learning, and well-being will be essential from preparation to orientation and induction and throughout their career.

TRANSFORMATIONS TO EDUCATOR PREPARATION PROGRAMS TO PREPARE TEACHER CANDIDATES FOR TEAMING

Teacher educators owe it to their teacher candidates to begin to prepare for the future. In our view, teacher educators, like ourselves, are preparing them to be advocates to work on teams and have a more flexible working environment and a more equitable learning environment. However, educator preparation programs (EPPs) are beholden to accreditors at the state- and national levels that prescribe requirements and standards affecting content, requirements, clinical practice, and the placement of teacher candidates with mentors.

While policymakers will need to be engaged to change some of the legislation around the more discrete policies related to teacher preparation and the workforce, there are some elements that can be transformed through strong school-university partnerships. EPPs and their school partners will need to work closely to align course content, clinical experiences, and the workplace in which educators will ultimately practice their profession.

Establishing School-University Partnerships

In the late 1990s, the educator preparation field began to focus on school-university partnerships. Partner schools, also known as professional development schools, were designed to strengthen four assets of the education system: educator preparation, professional development, curriculum development, and research and inquiry.[1] In many places, these models still exist and are as strong as ever. One of the primary tenets of these models was the simultaneous renewal of both the school and the university. This meant that universities could leverage assets to support and build new ways of teaching and learning and that schools would inform universities and break down the walls of the so-called ivory tower.

In most cases, these partnerships used teacher preparation as the "ground softener" for many new ideas, funded projects, and research. Not only did these partnerships prepare teacher candidates in better ways, but they also focused on school change for student learning as well. Placing teacher candidates on teams could ground-soften whole school Next Education Workforce models.

As schools and districts have partnered with us in redesigning staffing models, we have found school leaders and teachers interested in this change and have placed teacher candidates on grade level or vertical teams. In some cases, we have seen expansion of teams with teacher candidates (as opposed to paraprofessionals or aides), adding people to the core team of professional teachers. And in other cases, districts are using dollars for vacant positions to pay teacher candidates—but instead of putting them in their own classroom, they place them on a team.

Rethinking the Educator Preparation Program Curricular Components with Specialization and Advancement in Mind

EPPs will need to include specialization and advancement pathways. For instance, EPPs should include room for self-selected elective credit hours in their program's design. These elective credit hours might be connected to an endorsement area or, when stacked, signal a specialization. Teacher candidates may build these specializations based on their own interests or the needs of the populations they are considering serving.

In partnership with departments of education, EPPs will also need to think outside the box about how stackable credentials can lead to teacher certification. This allows EPPs to provide students—both those seeking degrees and those seeking stackable credentials—pathways that may make them more likely to persist in their EPP. Alternatively, a paraeducator might take two reading courses and receive a badge from an EPP that signifies that they have the knowledge and skills of a "reading accelerator." This may qualify them to work with small groups of students on particular topics or skills in reading. This allows them to remain in learning environments and continue their professional learning.

Rethinking Clinical Practice Experiences in Traditional Educator Preparation Programs

Four-year EPPs should include some type of professional practice each year. It will be important that programs practice working on teams and teaming early and often.

In their first and second years, teacher candidates intern in community organizations where working on teams is more prevalent. In these instances, not only do they begin to experience what it's like to work on a team, but they also see students learning in different environments, being held to different expectations, and beginning to understand distributed expertise. These organizations might be youth-serving nonprofits, museums, zoos, and other places.

They may also intern in schools where they can begin to work with students in team-based models, practicing the skills they are learning in their preparation program. A reading experience course might be taught at a school where teacher candidates learn a skill in the first hour, then work with small groups of students to practice the skill in the second hour, and then, in the third hour, teach the skill to other adults in the building (e.g., volunteers, parents, bus drivers, or office staff) to build the capacity of all adults in the school.

In their third year, teacher candidates may serve as interns one or two days per week, but they are given designated roles on a team and prepared as such. For example, students taking their math methods courses intern as math accelerators on teams and, in the second semester, become lab facilitators so they learn more about the power of AI-enhanced learning by monitoring student learning as they interact with technology.

Ultimately, the learning they are getting at the university is matched with experience but not just any experience—it's an explicit role that helps them develop and contribute as a team member. These roles would often be filled face-to-face but internships could also be in remote, digital learning environments. Rural communities could also take advantage of the supply and expertise of teacher candidates. Teacher candidates could also get a sense of "advancement" if credentials were provided that acknowledged learning along the way the skills that are developing. This also signals to schools and districts the abilities and roles teacher candidates can play along the way.

Finally, in their fourth year, teacher candidates should have a full-year clinical experience. Understanding, however, the tension and often inequity this creates for students who need a living income to support themselves and their families. This problem is alleviated when teacher candidates can be compensated. Yet, placing them, isolated, in their own classroom, underprepared, is problematic for the teacher candidate and for their students. Though, if EPPs and school districts consider teams, then teacher candidates can be placed in redesigned staffing models and have "just-right" responsibilities and gain the experience they need to thrive.

For instance, a school may have four third-grade positions. One is always hard to staff. A principal may work with district staff to decide that, going forward, third-grade staff will be staffed with three full-time teachers and three resident teachers. It is a restructuring of the school's staffing model: proactive, not reactive.

Rethinking Clinical Practice Experiences for Graduate and Alternative Certification Educator Preparation Programs

Graduate and alternative certification programs will also need to consider how to create experiences for teacher candidates, even though many are often hired as full-time instructor-of-record. In our view, none of these candidates (and they are still candidates) should be in classrooms by themselves. These individuals have varying skill levels and experience, but without a team, this could be a recipe for disaster.

Graduate residency models where a teacher candidate is paid and placed with a professional teacher for a year help address this somewhat—at least the teacher candidate/novice teacher is not in a classroom of their own. With teams and redesigned staffing models, residency models could scale in ways that don't rely on external funding and support. In addition, many of these candidates have prior lived experience that can now be shared as part of the distribution of expertise—a win-win.

Rethinking Mentoring in Clinical Experiences

While mentors are important, they are "only one component of a larger system that influences the student teaching experience, such as the general atmosphere or organizational culture in the internship school, the curriculum that student teachers experience, and so forth."[2] In acknowledging that there are a variety of other organizational characteristics that impact teacher candidate development, we believe that it is time to re-engage Ken Zeichner's impetus to "break outside the traditional structures of student teaching that have been with us for so many years."[3] By placing teacher candidates on teams, it provides teacher candidates with multiple "mentors" who have differing skill sets and prepares the next generation of teachers to actually work on teams and develop the mindset needed to change the system.

IN-SERVICE PROFESSIONAL LEARNING FOR TEAMS

The increasingly complex work of teaching requires that we build systems and structures beyond preservice preparation that address the realities of specific teaching contexts.[4] In response, education systems

continue to provide more and more professional development opportunities. The assumption that all teachers need to be "widget teachers"
who know and are able to do everything for students pushes us to "pile
on" professional learning. Just as there are lines around colleges of
education of well-meaning people who want more and more content in
teacher preparation, there are also those who believe that more professional learning is needed for all the content teachers didn't get in their
teacher preparation program.

Conventional professional learning opportunities, like professional
development days or enrolling in advanced university coursework, are
not suited to help teachers "transform complex knowledge and skills
into powerful teaching practices."[5] Most of the professional development is detached from natural contexts and from practice. As Richard
Elmore from the Harvard Graduate School of Education notes,

> there is almost no opportunity for teachers to engage in continuous and
> sustained learning about their practice in the settings in which they actu-
> ally work, observing and being observed by their colleagues in their own
> classrooms and classrooms of other teachers in other schools confronting
> similar problems.[6]

Moreover, as teachers leave or move, schools lose professional experience, institutional knowledge, and working relationships. The current
education workplace isn't designed to have embedded learning for new
and continuing professionals.

Teams are more than structural. It will be necessary to develop the
individual and collective decision-making of a team which requires the
types of dispositions—the collaborative nature, development of trust,
and collective ability to navigate uncertainty and conflict. Without
an intentional focus on developing these dispositions, there might be
another layer of complexity and difficulty to teaching by expecting
people to work in teams. Teams will need the practices necessary to
navigate relationships and engage in effective and healthy communication and dialogue, as well as develop the types of self-awareness
practices that make it possible for an individual to contribute and grow
effectively within the team and the relationships.

Therefore, there are at least two primary parts to professional learning for teaming. The first is the training of new skills, knowledge, and
dispositions. The other part is the ways in which the training happens.

Few of us went to school in team-based models. If Next Education Workforce models are going to be successfully implemented and sustained, there will need to be a lot of professional learning. This professional learning will need to be in a variety of modes: online and self-paced to provide basic content and understanding, through networked cohorts of teams who can share successes and challenges, and team-embedded self-improvement.

Understanding Teams and Teaming

Initially, educators will need to simply understand what we mean by teams and team-based teaching—what teams are and what they aren't. Educators will also need to understand what and how to distribute expertise, how to use space, how to flexibly group students, and how to be a team player. Team leaders will need additional training on how to lead teams, how to identify and distribute expertise, and how to lead co-planning sessions.

Creating Sustained Professional Learning Experiences

Teachers need sustained and substantive learning opportunities rather than superficial and episodic sessions. Rather than requiring that all teachers attend the same learning experiences, we should create protected and sustained opportunities for educator teams to come together and collaborate. Transitioning to Next Education Workforce models will require expert facilitators who understand how to move teams from baseline understandings of deeper learning, personalized learning, and teaming to robust application of these concepts.

Educator teams will need space and time to create communities of practice among their team and with other teams. These meetings might take place monthly via video conference to save educators travel time, energy, and money. Team members would attend the same sessions together, but the other teams attending might be from different schools and districts.

In these sustained sessions, educators can reflect on previously implemented plans and practices and explore new resources and instructional approaches. They should also have time to work as a team to create plans to implement what they are exploring and learning. Importantly, educators should have opportunities to celebrate successes and collaborate to solve challenges, within their team and across other teams.

Self-Improving Teams

Self-improving teams focus on the interactions of team members rather than particular actions made by a leader or a single teacher. They decide member tasks as a team and take collective responsibility for quality control, training, and performance feedback. It is valuable to have regular opportunities for teachers to come together, identify and work toward solving teaching dilemmas, and examine student learning patterns.

And, teachers do this regularly through professional learning communities. Though, researchers have suggested that, while teachers found it useful to share teaching "tips-and-tricks," pacing, and logistics, without additional support, they are "unlikely to support teachers in developing the perspectives and practices necessary for the engagement of a broad set of students."[7]

In self-improving teams, leadership is distributed and seen as interactions between team members. Based on expertise, teams decide what each member's tasks are. Teams see their learning experience delivery as a collective effort, take responsibility for it together, and provide feedback to one another when needed. Teaming allows educators to use their strengths to teach team members new knowledge and skills and for educators to learn in real time, rather than in isolated silos.

A whole new opportunity exists for those inclined to begin thinking about what these tools might look like and how schools will know if teams truly are self-improving and accomplishing what we want them to accomplish. How schools identify gaps in knowledge of the team will be critical as we learn more about the formation of teams, how they work together, and how they impact student learning.

CONCLUSION

To think about how to shift the mindset of an entire workforce and preparation for that workforce is daunting. Matching teacher preparation to the reality of the workplaces for which we are preparing teachers will be a bit of a balancing act. Until a critical mass of schools adopts team-based models, EPPs have to prepare graduates to succeed in one-teacher, one-classroom models even as they emphasize the skills, knowledge, and dispositions that will enable those graduates to thrive in teams.

To accomplish this, there will need to be changes to educator preparation by providing room for specializations, rethinking clinical experiences, and changes to mentoring. And, there will still be considerations as to how in-service educators are continually prepared for teaming. Teams will need professional learning experiences that help them build team culture including the practices and mindsets of distribute expertise, co-planning, co-instruction, assessment of deeper and personalized learning, and team leadership.

Teams of educators will also need the individual and collective autonomy to drive their professional learning so teams can be self-improving. However difficult, we believe these changes are actions that, we believe, have always been at the heart of what EPPs and school systems have wanted to do for a long time: creating enduring partnerships that lead to mutual improvement.

NOTES

1. Osguthorpe (1995).
2. Goldhaber et al. (2020, p. 588).
3. Zeichner (2002, p. 62).
4. Feiman-Nemser (2001).
5. Feiman-Nemser (2001, p. 1041).
6. Elmore (2004, p. 127).
7. Horn et al. (2018).

Chapter 9

Human Resource Systems to Support Team-Based Models

One of the most frequent questions we get is, "So, what are all the policy hurdles that get in the way of building team-based staffing models?" As it turns out, at the level of the nation and states, the answer is, "as of now, there aren't many." However, policies and, perhaps more importantly, inherited structures and processes at the level of the school system have big impacts on how successful team-based staffing models can be. To see the true power of teams of educators with distributed expertise, we must also transform how human capital management systems (HCMSs) function so that the right people can make strategic and evidence-based human resource (HR) decisions.

As more school systems move toward team-based models, we've seen increasing misalignment between their HCMS and strategic initiatives. They want students to engage in deeper and more personalized learning experiences, but that is difficult to accomplish in one-teacher, one-classroom models. Most hiring systems aren't designed to build teams by filtering job candidates based on their expertise and specializations. Instead, they are designed to find "the widget" elementary school teacher or "the widget" high school biology teacher.

Teachers are evaluated using observation instruments that are often oriented around teacher-centered instructional models and almost never account for team-based staffing. Additionally, in many of our current HCMSs, teachers are incentivized based on the achievement of their group of students. They are paid for their individual performance, which incentivizes isolation, rather than teamwork. If we want to create the conditions in which team-based models flourish, we must transform HCMSs so the default isn't hiring for, evaluating and incentivizing one-teacher, one-classroom models. Yes, we need accountability, but how we get there cannot be the responsibility of each individual.

TURQUOISE SCHOOL DISTRICT

Throughout this chapter, we will use Turquoise School District (TSD), which houses Trogon Elementary and Quail High, to illustrate how their HCMS is changing to adopting team-based staffing models. TSD has noticed some incongruities with its HCMS. For example, teacher evaluation processes are focused on the individual teacher with some components connected to a narrow definition of student academic performance.

Students' growth in the skills and dispositions aligned to the district's Portrait of a Graduate is missing from the teacher evaluation process. Additionally, these evaluation tools don't take into consideration the team of educators supporting student learning. TSD is thinking differently about how it designs, implements, utilizes, and evaluates its HCMS to align more with broader student outcomes and the district's commitment to team-based staffing models.

TRANSFORMATIONS TO DISTRICT-LEVEL HUMAN CAPITAL MANAGEMENT SYSTEMS

Education has paid relatively little attention to the hiring process. Many of the practices employed by HR professionals in education are compliance driven. Often, principals must sift through and review applicant after applicant, rather than receiving lists of potential candidates who may prove to be a good fit for a particular school or position. Some current policies demand that principals interview every current educator within a district who applies for a position at a particular school—a time-intensive task that is not a strategic use of leaders' time.

Schools should focus on building automated talent systems with integration of data, aligning recruitment and hiring practices to desired outcomes such as a Portrait of a Graduate. This is not an overnight process and will require districts to conduct a needs assessment that may lead to the creation of new data fields, queries, or reports that are capable of providing the information decision-makers need.

Hiring practices will also need to change. Primarily, we hire educators based on whether or not they meet basic certification requirements. Many hiring systems are not built to allow schools or teams to signal to human resources what essential areas of expertise they need in their learning environments. Nor do they allow candidates to specify their additional areas of expertise or strengths in ways that make it simple for HR professionals—or the system—to match those specialties to school and system needs.

Additionally, teachers themselves should play a larger role in the process of hiring educators who will join their teams. As better data systems collect information about the needs of schools and teams (beyond grade level or content area), schools should work with local teacher preparation program providers to identify candidates who have the specializations and emerging expertise that meets school hiring needs.

Lastly, creating viable pathways for high schoolers and resident teachers who want to join teams as professional educators will be essential. To make a residency sustainable, many school systems pay their resident teachers. Additionally, recruitment systems should allow for applicants to identify themselves as a former grow-your-own Teacher Academy student or a resident teacher who was on a team. This will allow districts to identify candidates that are likely to possess an understanding of a team, school, or district.

Transforming Turquoise School District Recruitment and Hiring

TSD plans to reassess its current HR practices and align them with the district goals and strategies. Of course, TSD will continue to screen applicants to ensure that they meet basic certification requirements. Additionally, however, they are working toward creating a system that allows applicants to identify their strengths and enables schools and teams to identify their needed areas of expertise. Applicants who are graduates of TSD's grow-your-own Teacher Academy program or former resident teachers will also be able to self-identify in the new system. Finally, TSD is considering how the funds for some of their chronically unfilled vacancies might be reallocated to pay resident teachers to work on teams.

CHANGES TO EDUCATOR
ROLES AND PATHWAYS

Effectively building educator teams with distributed expertise—beyond the widget teacher in a single classroom—will require changes to the way that roles and pipelines work within HCMSs. New roles for professional educators like lead teacher, school-based teacher educator, and cross-team curriculum designer will need to be formally built into HR systems.

More flexibility around whether roles are full- or part-time should also be built into the systems. As we move away from one-teacher, one-classroom models of schooling, the idea of a retired educator or a former teacher turned stay-at-home parent returning to the profession for ten to fifteen hours a week suddenly seems more plausible. HR systems need to be able to account for these scenarios. For new roles, teachers, principals, HR professionals, and other stakeholders will need to collaborate to determine key responsibilities associated with new roles and determine how they are selected, how they are evaluated, and how they access professional continuous professional learning.

HCMSs must also recognize, track, and reward substantive additional responsibilities that educators take on to make sure their teams address the needs of learners. Educators should be able to elect to take on meaningful responsibilities that come with stipends or with non-direct financial incentives, such as the time during the workday away from the learning environment.

Many of these systems already exist to recognize the time and service associated with activities like coaching sports, running clubs, and serving as a grade-level chair. It will be important not to over-complicate the system with dozens (or hundreds) of job-embedded responsibilities, but more should be done to formally recognize, and systematically operationalize, key roles that emerge as part of team-based staffing.

In addition to accommodating new roles, more flexible hours, and key responsibilities on teams, HCMSs also must do a better job working with new pathways into the education profession. Pathways for paraeducators and high school students in grow-your-own Teacher Academy programs are two viable options to potentially recruit a more diverse and durable educator workforce. Given the team-based structures, it will be increasingly possible for future professional educators to work as members of those teams with very specific responsibilities that can increase in scope along with their training.

For example, take paraeducators working in elementary schools. Many school systems and higher education partners are working to build pathways for paraeducators to become certified teachers. Currently, most of these systems operate as binaries—you are either a paraeducator or a classroom teacher.

Imagine an alternative: pathways could be built to prioritize all the courses related to teaching reading, and paraeducators, upon completing that sequence, could receive a new designation as a paraeducator with a literacy specialization and they would play an increased role in teaching reading in the team-based models. These educators, who are not yet credentialed professional teachers, could receive a different designation in the HCMS and receive an increase in hourly wage and/ or other incentives.

As systems leaders rethink their HCMSs, it will be important to identify the new pathways that exist and consider how team-based models might allow them more opportunities to think creatively about how those educators are tracked, recognized, and rewarded.

Changing Educator Roles and Pathways in Turquoise School District

TSD already has multiple grow-your-own Teacher Academies in its high schools and is working with a local teacher preparation program provider to map out a pathway for paraeducators. In consultation with educators and principals, TSD is creating new educator roles, both full- and part-time, such as lead teacher (responsible for effectively deploying the educator team given their goals) and cross-team curriculum designer (working across four teams to design project-based units for 60 percent of their time and spending the other 40 percent working with teams and students to implement those units). They will continue to use student data to identify what roles would meet the needs of students and what, if any, additional features will need to be present in the recruitment and hiring systems.

CHANGES TO SYSTEMS SUPPORTING AND RECOGNIZING PROFESSIONAL LEARNING

As school systems create staffing models organized around teams of educators with distributed expertise, the importance of having HCMSs that support and recognize expertise will become essential. Professional learning to improve educator effectiveness will need to be transformed to include the personalized needs of the educator and the needs of the team. As we have discussed in earlier chapters, professional learning can no longer be "sit-and-get" and isolated away from the learning environment. Instead, each educator should have access to personalized, professional learning that is job embedded.

School systems will need to consider how to recognize particular areas of expertise (e.g., digital badging or microcredentialing) and how it will be counted toward professional learning requirements, advancement opportunities, and more compensation. Currently, many systems still recognize "credit hours beyond a degree" or genericized continuing education units (CEUs).

Imagine a different world where educators could be incentivized to gain particular expertise in an area that was needed on their team. Imagine being able to post and hire for positions as a function of very particular skills that would complement those of the team. Educators could strategically upskill to access new and different roles and opportunities either on their own team or on other teams. The recruitment and hiring processes could become much more streamlined.

To operationalize the benefits associated with personalized professional learning, we need to get the grain size of the recognition right. If they are too big, most educators won't take them and they will be rife with the inequities that plague the current systems around advanced degrees (e.g., costly and time intensive). If they are too small, they will be meaningless, costly to authentically assess, and lack a signaling effect associated with outcomes.

Based on our experience, we think the right size is something that an educator could become skilled at in around ten to twelve hours. It feels strange putting hours into these because, ultimately, we believe they should be competency-based and be accomplished as fast as they can, but as slow as they must. Importantly, these units of professional learning should be stackable.

A New Educator Position

Imagine a new educator position called "lead teacher." The specifics can (and should) vary with context, but generally, they are responsible for leading the educator team and effectively deploying them to best personalize and deepen learning for all students. To be effective in this role, an educator needs particular expertise that might include upskilling in the following:

1. Building team culture
2. Setting team goals
3. Analyzing and responding to student data
4. Deploying the team to support learners
5. Productive conflict and crucial conversations
6. Supportive coaching strategies
7. Observing/evaluating team members (optional depending on context)
8. Hiring for distributed expertise (matrix-based team staffing)

One can imagine the authentic assessment associated with each of these topics. After having demonstrated effectiveness on those assessments, the educator would be recognized in the HCMS as having the expertise needed to be a "lead teacher" and they would be eligible to apply for that role on their team or other teams.

Tracking and recognizing personalized, stackable professional learning could be achieved with microcredentials and associated digital badges. The associated learning could be offered through local institutions of higher education, through other reputable microcredentialing platforms, or they might be created in-house within the school system. Ultimately, improving educational effectiveness in personalized ways for educators grants them more autonomy over their professional learning while also advancing equity by considering what professional learning to take based on the needs of their shared roster of students.

Supporting and Recognizing Professional Learning in Turquoise School District

TSD knows that teams will need guidance as they transition from one-teacher, one-classroom models to team-based staffing models. TSD also recognizes that teams can help to mitigate isolation and facilitate induction, especially for new teachers. TSD is working with the flagship state university to develop professional learning experiences, leveraging the university's assets and resources. The university is developing a multi-day gathering that helps guide educators to lay the groundwork for teaming and understanding tenants of deeper learning and personalized learning. In addition, the university is also considering how to create sustained professional development experiences that bring teams together to discuss problems of practice.

Finally, educators have the autonomy to identify their needs as educators and the needs of their students and engage in personalized, professional learning. TSD is working in-house and with the local teacher preparation program provider to develop microcredentials that educators can stack to acquire new specializations and work toward role advancement.

Changes to Evaluation and Incentives for Effective Educators and Teams

New evaluation and incentive structures will also be essential when building staffing models around educator teams. As districts provide more student-centered models of teaching and learning, they will likely need to move beyond narrowly using student achievement on standardized assessments as a means of evaluating and incentivizing educators and school leaders. This will involve the sourcing, or creation, of measurement tools, such as new observation instruments, student and educator surveys, and other ways to assess a much broader set of student and educator outcomes.

The foibles of most teacher evaluation systems are well documented—whether that be inflated observation ratings from administrators, measures of student achievement that are better proxies for family income, and others. The systems are well-intentioned but leave much to be desired. For example, even in today's normative one-teacher, one-classroom world, where multiple educators teach the same students, the share of students' outcomes that should be attributed to a single teacher is sometimes very complicated.

What is the contribution of the freshman biology teacher who has students read lots of nonfiction text and write multiple drafts of lab reports to the ELA teacher's nine-grade achievement scores? How much of the second-grade teachers' "excellent" rating in classroom management might actually be attributable to the seasoned paraeducator who spends 50 percent of her time in that classroom?

The point is, even in today's one-teacher, one-classroom models our ability to make an inference about an individual teacher's skill or impact is already compromised. Imagine what will happen when schools implement the sort of team-based models where educators are sharing common rosters of learners who are constantly being grouped and regrouped throughout the day and week. Our evaluation systems must account for the team-based nature of the work.

Because many of our educator incentive systems are based, at least in part, on the evaluation system, they too will need to change as systems adopt team-based staffing models. Currently, many of our HCMSs reward individuals for their performance. These systems perpetuate one-teacher, one-classroom models by failing to recognize teacher teamwork and collaboration.

In addition to utilizing redesigned educator evaluation systems that acknowledge team-based models and include broader student outcomes, school systems should also consider *team* incentives, which are common in other fields. In the short term, these incentives would complement existing individual incentive structures. Team performance should be incentivized and educators should be able to collectively plan to use this team-based incentive as the team sees fit, again, returning autonomy to the educators.

We know that teachers in the United States spend, on average, about $450 per year on their classrooms. Imagine if there were team-based incentives that equaled $500 × the number of core educators on a team? Having a team budget that would save them from dipping into their personal savings might go a long way to both giving educators the respect they deserve as professionals and incentivizing strong team culture and commitment to shared outcomes.

Changes to Evaluation and Incentives for Effective Educators and Teams in Turquoise School District

TSD is allocating funds for incentives for their lead teachers. In collaboration with educators and principals, they are creating the job responsibilities, selection process and criteria, evaluation system, and how these lead teachers will be trained. TSD is creating an in-house professional learning series for potential lead teachers.

TSD is also aligning its teacher evaluation with its Portrait of a Graduate. It will now consider broader indicators, beyond solely measuring student outcomes with test scores, and include observation instruments that are team-level (as opposed to teacher-level). TSD believes that a change in evaluation culture that values and incentivizes collaboration will increase the coordination and collaboration among teachers. Finally, TSD will grant incentives to teams, based on their team-level performance on these new indicators. Teams will have the autonomy to use their team incentive in the ways they see fit for the needs of their team or learners, with guidelines co-constructed between teams, principals, and district staff.

SCHOOL-LEVEL FISCAL STRATEGIES FOR TEAM-BASED STAFFING MODELS

Whether it is team-based incentives, stipends for new responsibilities, or new positions all together, many administrators hear about the team-based staffing models that we've described so far and immediately think they will be more expensive. They certainly could be. And, given funding for American education, probably should be. Systems and schools who are building these team-based models have found, however, that there are not necessarily increased costs, but *tradeoffs* that they must make. Examples from Trogon Elementary and Quail High School demonstrate this point.

Financial Strategies at Trogon Elementary

Principal Olmos is considering new financial models as he builds Next Education Workforce models at Trogon Elementary. To do this, he makes shifts in funding at his school. Principal Olmos reduced four full-time positions in grades K-3 that were unfilled or hard to staff each year. In doing this, he saved $53,000 per teacher or a total saving of $212,000.

Principal Olmos has also decided that he wants to work with the local teachers college to lead in-school and in-team professional development experiences. At the school level, he is saving $40,000 on professional development by making this transition (and, consider how much more TSD would save as a whole if implemented at the district level). In total, Principal Olmos is saving $252,000.

He wants to reallocate $229,000 of his $252,000 savings to pay the following:

• Eight resident teachers: Stipends of $15,000 each for a total of $120,000.

- Two lead teachers: Stipend of $5,000 each for a total of $10,000.
- A learning disability teacher: Salary of $75,000.
- Two community educators: Salary of $12,000 each for a total of $24,000.

Student Teacher Ratios

Since Principal Olmos has employed resident teachers, he did not increase his student-to-teacher ratios. In fact, his ratio decreased from 16:1 to 13:1 when paraeducators, resident teachers, and professional educators were considered.

Weekly Rotating Learning Blocks

To ensure that educators have ample collaborative planning time, Principal Olmos created weekly project-based learning blocks for the Trogon students, which are led by the librarian and media specialist teachers, in addition to support from specials teachers, paraeducators, and community educators. His previous budgetary shifts allow for compensation for the community educators. Now, every Friday, each core instructional team has around two and a half hours of collaborative planning time. K-1 teams plan in the morning, 2-3 teams in the middle of the day, and 4-6 teams plan in the afternoon.

Additional Strategy: Repurpose Substitute Allocations

Rather than supplying one substitute for one classroom when an educator is absent, the team is able to regroup students and cover for their missing teammate. This allows for the consistency of adults that are educating the students but also saves around $48,000 (or around $6,000 per team) to be reconsidered for other roles in his team-based model. He might hire a part-time project-based curriculum designer that facilitates the weekly learning block or potentially more community educators.

Financial Strategies at Quail High School

Principal Okpara at Quail High wants to make financial changes to sustain her Next Education Workforce models. Recognizing that two electives, woodshop and personal finance, have consistently lower class sizes than other elective choices, Principal Okpara wants to remove these as electives and bring in community educators to integrate these content areas into the project-based portions of students' weeks. She removes woodshop and personal finances as two full-time positions, which cost $56,000 each, saving a total of $112,000.

Principal Okpara wants to reallocate this funding to pay lead teachers and community educators. Specifically, she wants to pay the following:

- Eight lead teachers: Stipend of $5,000 for a total of $40,000.
- Six community educators: Stipend of $12,000 each for a total of $72,000.

In total, she is saving $112,000 by reducing two teachers and reinvesting the $112,000 to bring more community educators into Quail's team-based model while also creating new advancement pathways for educators.

Stacking Teaching Time

Principal Okpara decides to stack instructional time for multiple teams to create more planning time. This means, for instance, that her ninth-grade core Arts Team and Sustainability Team teach in the morning, and, while the students attend their electives in the afternoon, those teams have co-planning time. The other teams have the inverse of this (co-planning in the morning while students are in electives, teach in the afternoon) or a split (teach in the morning, co-plan in part of the morning and part of afternoon while students are in electives, teach again the afternoon). Ultimately, she remains cost neutral in her investments and shifts.

Additional Strategies: Repurpose Funds by Reducing Other Positions.

Principal Okpara also considers reducing positions in the schools that could be split or redeployed, such as administrators, instructional assistants, academic supports, and media specialists.

Regrouping within Team to Increase Planning Time.

Principal Okpara considers that lead teachers might need time to prepare for team meetings. She considers adding an inquiry/project-based learning block on Wednesdays—which the core educator team covers—at the end of student-centered content instruction so that all team leads can meet together.

CONCLUSION

In education, HCMSs are designed to perpetuate one-teacher, one-classroom models, not only through hiring but through evaluation and incentive processes as well. Building team-based models will require substantial coordination and collaboration between educators, administrators, and HR professionals. The examples throughout this chapter highlight how school districts have made team-based models financially sustainable; they have made trade-offs and reallocated their resources. Redesigning HCMSs is not an easy feat; however, doing so will help ensure the impact and long-term sustainability of team-based models.

Chapter 10

Optimism and Systems Change

We have heard a lot from people in all facets of the system. Many have the desire to move to systems that make sense and achieve the purpose for kids and adults in schools, but there is pessimism about the how. To expect that the solutions to the grand challenges of education will be discovered if we continue to root them in the same one-teacher, one-classroom model that we've had for decades is, we argue, inconceivable.

There are great things being built: curricular innovation, technological solutions, many products, and programs with real potential. However, many are not feasible or as robust as they could be in the current system. Teachers can't take on one more thing by themselves. They need a team. They need others with differing skill levels and skill sets that they can lean on, delegate to, and learn from. If we started to think about solutions for teams, personalized and deeper learning, and specializations and advancement, then maybe our solutions would be different—and would actually push the systems to change, to be more equitable, and to be more sustainable in the long run.

Throughout this book, we provide the hope and optimism that we believe teaming can bring. While we recognize that there are many moving parts to this, we also think if enough schools, districts, policymakers, funders, and higher education institutions came together, we could create better working conditions for educators and better learning environments for students—equitable outcomes for both teachers and students.

Teaching is a complex activity with events that are multidimensional, simultaneous, and unpredictable. Teaming helps break down this complex activity into manageable parts. It has the possibility of decreasing both the cognitive load of teachers and the feelings of being overwhelmed by the amount of simultaneous activity that happens in the classroom. It provides flexibility when a teacher needs to be absent. By placing novice teachers on teams with experienced educators, mentorship and coaching can happen in real-time, breaking down the structural isolation that teachers report feeling in one-teacher, one-classroom models.

All team members improve by working together with others who have differing experiences and expertise. Teams support paraeducators by helping them move from generalists to technicians with specific skills to play both general and specific roles on teams. Community educators' presence in learning environments helps to broaden perceptions of "who can be an educator" and allows for a greater diversity of people to surround them.

Through teaming, we can start to provide students with the deeper and personalized learning experiences that they need to be academically and socially successful. In addition to academic outcomes, there are potential social benefits to team-based instruction. These teams can be instrumental in increasing students' social capital, or their access to—and ability to mobilize—relationships to further their potential and goals.

Teams increase the quantity of relationships, bettering the chance of finding the support they need; the quality of relationships, the extent to which those relationships with educators meet their relational, developmental, and instructional needs; the structure of networks allowing students to see how educators are connected in professional and personal ways aligning with their own interests; and the ability to mobilize relationships, how to use the right people at the right time. More educators mean more eyes on students. More educators mean more perspectives about the strengths of students and ways to better appreciate them and their unique needs.

FUTURE DIRECTIONS FOR RESEARCH

Education researchers have provided evidence and thought leadership for years about the benefits of teacher collaboration, distributed leadership, professional learning communities, and multi-classroom leaders. We know the opportunities students have by engaging in personalized and deeper learning such as problem-based or project-based learning. We understand the advantages of building social capital, agency, and self-efficacy for both adults and students. The list goes on as we look at best practices in teaching in the disciplines.

And when we looked at all of it, we arrived at our anchor statement: if we want more equitable educational outcomes, we need to build teams of educators with distributed expertise who can deepen and personalize learning for all students; and with this approach, we create better ways to enter, specialize, and advance in the profession.

Now, we need more research about how these models are built, how they function, and whether the benefits we believe, based on current literature, hold true in practice. We need to examine the models, educators, and learners. The table below gives a glimpse at the research questions we are beginning to ask and explore a number of interim outcomes.

Models

- *Essential Elements*: What are the defining elements of Next Education Workforce models? Are particular elements more important at different stages?
- *Implementation*: How are models implemented?
- *Transformation*: How do schools and systems move toward sustainable Next Education Workforce models?

Educators

- *Efficacy*: Are educators in Next Education Workforce models more effective?
- *Diversity*: To what degree are Next Education Workforce models associated with educator diversity?
- *Professional Satisfaction*: How do models affect recruitment, retention, and job satisfaction? Are teachers who teach in teams more likely to stay in the profession, be satisfied in their jobs, and feel more supported?

Learners

- *Academic Growth*: What are the effects of models on academic outcomes?
- *Socio-emotional Growth*: What are the effects of models on social, emotional, motivational, and cognitive skills?

- *Social Capital Formation*: How do models affect students' access to diverse social networks?
- *Equity Indicators*: How do models narrow the disparities? How do models increase learning outcomes, wellness outcomes?

All the past research is relevant to the synergy we are trying to capture here. We begin with early research on teams, teaming, co-teaching, distributed leadership, and more. We will also need recommendations for schools and school systems about how to build systems to track efficacy and effective implementation; the costs to kids will be high if people do not adjust and fine-tune as they go. We need to consider what data systems might need to be built, accountability structures, and feedback loops with teachers, learners, and families. All of these are not necessarily equal, and logic models need to be built so we can test what's most important for student welfare—supports for academic, socio-emotional, and more.

It will take time to understand the differential impacts of Next Education Workforce models on teachers and on students. However, our early findings are creating optimism. Teachers who participate in Next Education Workforce models are reporting increased team culture, practices related to deeper learning and personalized learning experiences, equity for learners, and personal and organizational benefits.

WHERE TO BEGIN

Reimagining the education workforce for the twenty-first century will require strong partnerships held together by the kind of resilient trust that allows people and institutions to share collaborative risk. Partners need to include policymakers, P-12 school and school district leaders, business leaders, youth-serving nonprofit leaders, and others. An education workforce for the twenty-first century will only succeed if the teaching and learning environment becomes a focus of the entire community. Designing a more effective education workforce is a civil society challenge that requires a civil society response. We need to build partnerships that address educational policy, the relationship between education and economic health, and the social dimensions of the communities in which our schools sit.

What Schools and Districts Can Do

All of this can be overwhelming and in an intractable field hard to know where to begin. You can't do all of it at once. Our suggestion: find a great school leader—elementary, middle, or secondary—who gets these ideas and is really ready for change. Let them know they have the support to move this forward and for long enough to make it stick and see results. Ask them to identify one or two groups of teachers also ready for change and who work together well. Get going! Find more leaders, find more teams and build whole school models. It will catch on. Then, you'll need to build the human capital systems to support it, but you will see exactly what you need as schools build.

To help, we have identified four stages of transformation to team-based staffing models: Exploring, Launching, Expanding, and Sustaining.

- *Exploring.* In the exploring phase, schools are interested in learning more about Next Education Workforce models and might already be experimenting with teaming, such as a resident team. They may also be laying the foundation for learner-centered models of instruction. A district may identify a school that they believe is ready to launch this model.
- *Launching.* A school may pilot a small number of teams.
- *Expanding.* A school expands its whole school to Next Education Workforce models. They focus on adding additional teams as readiness and resources allow.
- *Sustaining.* Schools continue to refine the ways they support students and educators in their Next Education Workforce model.

Now, imagine 100 or even 500 districts starting to move in this direction—exploring, launching, expanding, and sustaining—that's at least the same number of schools and teams but exponentially moving in the same direction, we could have a large movement in a short period of time. In designing how educators work and work together, we should strive to rethink the responsibilities and loads of individuals so that educators have more flexibility and room for creativity.

We also need to think about what accountability means for teams, not just for individuals, and what that means for educator evaluation and career pathing. Exposure to a more diverse array of colleagues who bring different strengths and skills to the team should provide educators with a more intellectually rewarding work environment, more leadership opportunities, and more routes to consider as they design their own professional growth paths. Finally, there are, of course, funding and compensation implications. The right question isn't "Will this cost more than the model we've been living with?" because that model has, with a few local exceptions, still been underfunded. Yet, we should explore differentiated pay for different roles and what can be done that is cost neutral.

What Policymakers Can Do

How do we identify and achieve the outcomes that would let policymakers trust educators and work with them instead of thinking their job is just to police educators? The underlying causes of the teacher shortage affect public, charter, and private schools. All schools—and all school models—are concerned with attracting and retaining an effective workforce. Policies that restrict the entry of educators into the system don't allow for creativity in attracting and developing talent, and policies that open up the system without intentionality, perhaps simply to address an emergency need for staff regardless of qualifications, often degrade the quality of education children receive and the ability of a system to retain effective educators.

Too many policies, however, well intentioned, simply get in the way of the ability of educators to deliver good outcomes for kids. Policy is also often contradictory and too often driven by anecdote rather than data. Policymakers will need to come to a much better appreciation of the reality that context matters. A policy that works for learners in one context may, in fact, harm learners in another context. A successful reimagination of the education workforce will need champions and partners in the policy world who will work with educators to effect context-aware systemic change rather than palliative measures.

We need policymakers willing to examine existing policies and remove what's getting in the way of enacting new structures. Policymakers need to support the whole education system and create policies and incentives that boost creativity and outcomes for all. Any serious discussion of education workforce design will have to lucidly address issues of funding, access, and equity.

What the Business Community Can Do

It's time for the business community and the education community to redesign their relationship into a true working partnership. Businesses need to view education systems as something more than a source of labor, and educators need to view businesses as something more than a source of material resources. Businesses should be willing to partner in ways that immerse them in the systems of schools so that they can bring their expertise to the table. And business leaders need to cultivate an openness to understanding the complexities of education in the same way they understand the complexities of their own sectors.

Education leaders should be open to what they can learn from other industries to inform the education workforce. We've only scratched the surface. Business leaders from other sectors have experience in complex organizational design and, if brought into the work in an intentional manner, can add insight into how we redesign and deploy educators.

What Education Preparation Programs Can Do

Needless to say, the implications for educator preparation of reimagining the education workforce are immense. If we want educators who can work at different social and organizational scales, with individual learners and peers, with parents and community organizations, and with partners in both the private and public sectors—if we want all that, we need to cultivate some habits of mind and dispositions in educators.

First, we have to think through what the student experience looks like and how our systems of preparation need to change to address that and a new school experience. Systemic issues that are part of the conversation include certification, evaluation, and how we look at student outcomes and expectations. If schools are expected to be places where we introduce children to the idea and practice of civil society, the education workplace should be a more robust reflection of civil society. Diversifying the workforce, changing organizational structures, and increasing opportunities for graduated pay are all ways of making education more attractive to teachers, students, families, and community organizations and businesses.

Educator preparation should find ways to break their own siloed systems and develop educators as team members who can ask the right questions, navigate uncertainty, and work to design and create solutions to the toughest challenges, especially as we move toward more personalized and deeper learning approaches. They need to become models for what learning environments could look like. Providing personalized learning for educator candidates will help those candidates see how they can personalize learning for younger students.

They should also be thinking about their partnerships and how they can leverage their assets—teacher candidates and faculty—to enact change in schools through requiring team-based clinical experiences. How does education preparation break out of the "take all your coursework, then do your clinical practice" model of preparation? What is the right mix and sequence of experiences we need to provide to teacher candidates? How do we provide voice and choice to differentiate the preparation experience based on the teacher candidate's experience and expertise?

BUILDING GUARDRAILS

There are always potential risks in building team-based models, so our guardrails need to be strong. We cannot de-professionalize the profession by relying too much on community educators or those not fully prepared as professional teachers. We need to be careful that in our zeal for diversifying our workforce, we do not end up with a class system where teachers of color fill less-than-professional ranks. We need to ensure that, when building teams, we attend to the team's culture. We need to ensure that we build systems that do not let learners fall through the cracks, although this happens too often in today's one-teacher, one-classrooms models. We have to stay with this long enough to see if there is improvement and impact we're looking for; it will take time for the whole system to shift and going back will always seem easier.

We believe that there are some first steps we can take today that don't cost a lot of money. In fact, school systems could reallocate money with better purpose, and utilizing and retaining the current workforce. We don't have to overcomplicate this—we just need to find the willing and provide some autonomy and time so they can figure it out. We still have a lot to learn about teams and how they can better support learners, but we know a lot too from colleagues in education disciplines like special education and from other fields like healthcare and business, where teaming has been critical.

FINAL MESSAGE

There is so much to do, and our learners can't wait. Too few see education as a viable career path and too many are leaving too quickly. Too many students are not getting the education they need or deserve for our economy, democracy, or equitable outcomes. There is no one-size-fits-all approach to the Next Education Workforce, and we understand completely that context matters. We are not being prescriptive about a model, and we hope we've made that clear. Rather, we are exploring the ways that school systems and schools are building, testing, trying, and changing how educators work together, learn together, and serve students in the best ways with the best practices.

We want to fundamentally change the system so that more people see teaching as a viable profession; more parents tell their kids that teaching is a noble, honorable, and enjoyable professional path; and a diversity of people see the profession as a community that is inclusive and welcoming. The educators in the Next Education Workforce will need to be nimble, flexible, and dynamic.

Changes to the system have to happen at the speed of trust, but we simply can't wait any longer. After decades of school reform, the structure or systems of education have changed very little, especially the ways in which teachers function and the roles they play. Technology is upon us like never before, and the world is changing too quickly for the one-teacher, one-classroom model where a teacher needs to know and be able to do everything learners need them to do. It's just not sustainable. We need the Next Education Workforce.

Bibliography

Aguliar, E. (2013, January 28). Deeper learning means educational equity in urban schools. *Edutopia*. https://www.edutopia.org/blog/deeper-learning-educational-equity-urban-school-elena-aguilar

Arizona State University. (n.d.). *Cost of college and financial aid for graduate students*. Retrieved January 25, 2022. https://admission.asu.edu/aid/graduate

Audrain, R. L., Weinberg, A. E., Bennett, A., O'Reilly, J., & Basile, C. G. (2022). Ambitious and sustainable post-pandemic workplace design for teachers: A portrait of the Arizona teacher workforce. In F. M. Reimers (Ed.), *Primary and secondary education during covid-19: Disruptions to educational opportunity during a pandemic* (pp. 353–381). Springer International Publishing. https://doi.org/10.1007/978-3-030-81500-4_14

Batruch, A., Autin, F., Bataillard, F., & Butera, F. (2019). School selection and the social class divide: How tracking contributes to the reproduction of inequalities. *Personality and Social Psychology Bulletin*, *45*(3), 477–490. https://doi.org/10.1177/0146167218791804

Boveda, M., & Weinberg, A. E. (2020). Facilitating intersectionally conscious collaborations in physics education. *The Physics Teacher*, *58*(7), 480–483. https://doi.org/10.1119/10.0002066

Bureau of Labor Statistics. (2022). Occupational outlook handbook, teacher assistant. U.S. Department of Labor. https://www.bls.gov/ooh/education-training-and-library/teacher-assistants.html

Carver-Thomas, D. (2018). *Diversifying the teaching profession: How to recruit and retain teachers of color*. Learning Policy Institute. https://doi.org/10.54300/559.310

Charania, M., & Fisher, J. F. (2020). *The missing metrics: Emerging practices for measuring students' relationships and networks* (p. 29). Christensen Institute. https://www.christenseninstitute.org/wp-content/uploads/2020/07/THE-MISSING-METRICS.pdf

Cuban, L. (2018, December 9). Whatever happened to team teaching? *Larry Cuban on School Reform and Classroom Practice*. https://larrycuban .wordpress.com/2018/12/09/whatever-happened-to-team-teaching/

Darling-Hammond, L. (2001). The challenge of staffing our schools. *Educational Leadership, 58*(8).

Darling-Hammond, L., & Oakes, J. (2019). *Preparing teachers for deeper learning*. Harvard Education Press.

Education Commission. (2020). *Transforming the education workforce: Learning teams for a learning generation*. https://educationcommission.org /wp-content/uploads/2019/09/Transforming-the-Education-Workforce-Full -Report.pdf

Elmore, R. F. (2004). *School reform from the inside out: Policy, practice, and performance*. Harvard Education Press.

Every Student Succeeds Act, 20 U.S.C. § 6301. (2015). https://www.congress .gov/bill/114th-congress/senate-bill/1177

Feiman-Nemser, S. (2001). From preparation to practice: Designing a continuum to strengthen and sustain teaching. *Teachers College Record, 103*(6), 1013–1055. https.//doi.org/10.1111/0161-4681.00141

Gallup. (2017, June 8). How to keep kids excited about school. *Gallup. Com.* https://news.gallup.com/opinion/gallup/211886/keep-kids-excited -school.aspx

Goldhaber, D., Krieg, J., Naito, N., & Theobald, R. (2020). Making the most of student teaching: The importance of mentors and scope for change. *Education Finance and Policy, 15*(3), 581–591. https://doi.org/10.1162/edfp_a _00305

Goldring, R., & Taie, S. (2018). *Principal attrition and mobility: Results from the 2016-17 principal follow-up survey: First look*. U.S. Department of Education.

Greene, P. (2019, September 5). We need to stop talking about the teacher shortage. *Forbes*. https://www.forbes.com/sites/petergreene/2019/09/05/we -need-to-stop-talking-about-the-teacher-shortage/

Hassel, E. A., & Hassel, B. C. (2021). *Opportunity anew: How excellent educators can lift up their colleagues, students, and the nation in the wake of covid-19* (p. 7). Opportunity Culture. https://files.eric.ed.gov/fulltext/ ED611546.pdf

Hewlett Foundation. (2013). *Deeper learning competencies*. https://hewlett.org /wp-content/uploads/2016/08/Deeper_Learning_Defined__April_2013.pdf

Horn, I. S., Kane, B. D., & Garner, B. (2018). Teacher collaborative time: Helping teachers make sense of ambitious teaching in the context of their schools. In P. Cobb, C. Jackson, E. Henrick, & T. M. Smith (Eds.), *Systems for instructional improvement: Creating coherence from the classroom to the district office* (pp. 93–112). Harvard Education Press.

Ingersoll, R. M., May, H., & Collins, G. (2017). *Minority teacher recruitment, employment, and retention: 1987 to 2013.* Learning Policy Institute. https://repository.upenn.edu/gse_pubs/496

Ingersoll, R., Merrill, L., & May, H. (2014). *What are the effects of teacher education and preparation on beginning teacher attrition?* (p. 40). Consortium for Policy Research in Education. https://www.cpre.org/sites/default/files/researchreport/2018_prepeffects2014.pdf

Ingersoll, R. M., Merrill, E., Stuckey, D., & Collins, G. (2018). *Seven trends: The transformation of the teaching force – Updated October 2018* (CPRE Research Reports). Consortium for Policy Research in Education. https://repository.upenn.edu/cpre_researchreports/108

Ingersoll, R. M., & Strong, M. (2011). The impact of induction and mentoring Programs for beginning teachers: A critical review of the research. *Review of Educational Research, 81*(2), 201–233. https://doi.org/10.3102/0034654311403323

Kane, T. J., Rockoff, J. E., & Staiger, D. O. (2008). What does certification tell us about teacher effectiveness? Evidence from New York City. *Economics of Education Review, 27*(6), 615–631. https://doi.org/10.1016/j.econedurev.2007.05.005

Mary Lou Fulton Teachers College, Arizona State University. (2019). *Principled innovation in the systems of educator and leader preparation.* https://education.asu.edu/sites/default/files/framework-for-principled-innovation.pdf

McCardle, T. (2020). A critical historical examination of tracking as a method for maintaining racial segregation. *Educational Considerations, 45*(2). https://doi.org/10.4148/0146-9282.2186

Northern, A. M. (2020, July 7). *A snapshot of substitute teaching in the U.S.* The Thomas B. Fordham Institute. https://fordhaminstitute.org/national/commentary/snapshot-substitute-teaching-us

Osguthorpe, R. T. (Ed.). (1995). *Partner schools: Centers for educational renewal* (1st ed.). Jossey-Bass Publishers.

Pane, J., Steiner, E., Baird, M., & Hamilton, L. (2015). *Continued progress: Promising evidence on personalized learning.* RAND Corporation. https://doi.org/10.7249/RR1365

Partelow, L. (2019, December 3). What to make of declining enrollment in teacher preparation programs. *Center for American Progress.* https://www.americanprogress.org/article/make-declining-enrollment-teacher-preparation-programs/

Patrick, S., Kennedy, K., & Powell, A. (2013). *Mean what you say: Defining and integrating personalized, blended and competency education.* International Association for K-12 Online Learning. https://files.eric.ed.gov/fulltext/ED561301.pdf

Phi Delta Kappa International. (2018). *Teaching: Respect but dwindling appeal* (The 50th Annual of the Public's Attitudes Toward the Public Schools). https://pdkpoll.org/wp-content/uploads/2020/05/pdkpoll50_2018.pdf

Ricigliano, R. (2021, September 27). *The complexity spectrum.* https://blog .kumu.io/the-complexity-spectrum-e12efae133b0

Robinson, W. (2017). Teacher education: A historical overview. In D. Clandinin & J. Husu (Eds.), *The Sage handbook of research on teacher education* (pp. 49–67). SAGE Publications Ltd. https://doi.org/10.4135 /9781526402042.n3

The School Superintendents Association [AASA]. (2021). *An American imperative: A new vision of public schools.* http://aasacentral.org/wp-content /uploads/2021/04/CommissionReportFINAL_040821.pdf

Spillane, J. P. (2005). Distributed leadership. *The Educational Forum, 69*(2), 143–150. https://doi.org/10.1080/00131720508984678

Trump, J. L., & Miller, D. F. (1968). *Secondary school improvement: Proposal and procedures.* Allyn and Bacon, Inc.

Vialet, J., & Moos, A. von. (2020). *Substantial classrooms: Redesigning the substitute teaching experience.* Jossey-Bass.

Weisberg, D., Sexton, S., Mulhern, J., & Keeling, D. (2009). *The widget effect: Our national failure to acknowledge and act on differences in teacher effectiveness.* The New Teacher Project. https://tntp.org/assets/documents/ TheWidgetEffect_2nd_ed.pdf

World Health Organization. (2007). *Task shifting: Rational redistribution of tasks among health workforce teams: Global recommendations and guide-lines.* https://www.who.int/healthsystems/TTR-TaskShifting.pdf

Zeichner, K. (2002). Beyond traditional structures of student teaching. *Teacher Education Quarterly, 29*(2), 59–64.

About the Authors

Carole G. Basile is the dean of the Mary Lou Fulton Teachers College at Arizona State University (ASU). Prior to joining ASU, Basile was dean and professor in the college of education at the University of Missouri St. Louis (UMSL). As dean at ASU, her work has centered on redesigning the education workforce and changing practices in teacher and leadership preparation. She is currently working with education organizations nationally and internationally to design new systems for educators and their students and enable organizational change in this area. She is recognized for her work in math and science education, teacher education, and environmental education and has published numerous articles, books, book chapters, and technical papers. Her prior work includes *A Good Little School* and *Intellectual Capital: The Intangible Assets of Professional Development Schools.*

Her community work is extensive as she has actively partnered with many schools and school districts, community and youth-serving organizations, and businesses to create access and opportunity for all children and youth. She serves on the board of Education Reimagined, American Association of Colleges for Teacher Education, and Teach for America Phoenix. She also has prior experience in the areas of sales, management, corporate training, and human capital development.

Brent W. Maddin is executive director of the Next Education Workforce where he collaborates with colleagues across Arizona State University (ASU), P12 educators, and the community to redesign models of schooling based on teams of educators with distributed expertise who are better able to deliver on the promise of deeper and personalized learning for all students. Additionally, these team-based models help address many of the reasons educators leave the profession by creating more equitable and sustainable ways to enter, specialize, and advance in the profession. Prior to coming to ASU, Brent was cofounder and provost at the Relay Graduate School of Education where he set the curricular vision for the institution and managed teams focused on curriculum design, institutional research, and programmatic innovation. While at Relay, Brent also founded TeacherSquared—a national center dedicated to increasing collaboration among teacher preparation institutions. Prior to helping launch TeacherSquared and Relay, Brent earned a doctorate from the Harvard Graduate School of Education, served as a founding staff member at IDEA College Prep, and was a National Board Certified Teacher in secondary science.

R. Lennon Audrain (Richard "Lennon" Audrain) is a PhD student in educational policy and evaluation in the Mary Lou Fulton Teachers College at ASU. Prior to pursuing his doctorate, Lennon taught Latin, Spanish, and English in Arizona and Massachusetts and was the former national president of Educators Rising. Lennon's research explores teacher recruitment and teacher preparation. In particular, he looks at high school–based grow-your-own teacher programs, more commonly known as Teacher Academies, and community college teacher education programs. He investigates their program designs, credentials received after program completion, and articulation to other programs. Lennon earned his bachelor's degree in classics, concentrating in Latin, and his first master's degree in curriculum and instruction, both from ASU, and his second master's degree in technology, innovation, and education from the Harvard Graduate School of Education.